eat
smart

NIOMI SMART

This book is dedicated to you.

You, who have been there since day one,
and who have followed me on my journey every
step of the way, and you, who have picked up
this book, and decided to give me a chance.

Without you I wouldn't be where I am
today. I am lucky to have subscribers,
followers, readers, and friends, and I couldn't
be happier that you are one of them.

Thank you for listening to me, trying my
recipes, and hopefully being inspired.

Thank you for making this book possible.

Niomi

eat
smart

**what to eat in a day
—every day**

NIOMI SMART

STERLING EPICURE
New York

CONTENTS

WELCOME

Welcome to *Eat Smart*! I'm Niomi Smart, a lifestyle blogger and cofounder of the healthy snack boxes SourcedBox. After transitioning to a plant-based diet in 2014, I started to create my own recipes and share them with my audience on my Instagram, YouTube channel, and blog. Some of my most popular videos have been my "What I Eat in a Day" series, where I showcase all the delicious meals I have throughout the day. This has inspired the structure of *Eat Smart*. People seemed to really enjoy them and kept asking me for more, so I set myself a goal to write my own recipe book.

One thing you should know before we get started is that *Eat Smart* is in no way a diet book; it's a healthy cookbook and contains delicious recipes, all made from natural ingredients that do wonders for your health. Rather than putting you on a fad diet and restricting your food options, this book will help you learn to love your fresh fruit and vegetables and find easy, accessible recipes that you can incorporate into your busy life.

If you, like me, really notice the benefits of eating this way, you may find yourself also adopting a fully plant-based way of eating, or you may be happy with your overall diet, but simply wish to include one or two plant-based healthy meals during the week. Whatever reason you picked up this book, I truly hope you enjoy every recipe, and can tell how much thought and love I have put into it.

ABOUT ME

In 2010, I went to university to study law, intending to pursue a career as a lawyer. I loved studying the legal system, but I realized near the end of my final year that practicing law was a whole other story and that this path wasn't for me. When I graduated, it was a period of feeling proud and having a huge sense of accomplishment, after years of hard work. Yet, at the same time, I felt a sense of fear that I was now released into the adult world and expected to skip down the perfectly clear, yellow brick road that was my career, when actually it wasn't what I wanted. I created a blog in 2013, a couple of months after I graduated, because I found I had so many different passions outside of my law degree that I needed to have my own outlet, where I could express myself in other ways, mainly focusing on beauty and fashion.

After a few months, I decided to also start my YouTube channel, where I could really connect with my audience, which had grown on my blog. It was around this time that I discovered the importance of eating well, and that's when I found I was most passionate about making videos about health and well-being. I realized that healthy food doesn't have to be bland, and can, in fact, be fun and creative.

I would often Instagram my food, and people would ask for the recipes. That's when my "What I Eat in a Day" videos were born. These videos range from what I eat, when I'm traveling in places such as Bali, to what I eat when I'm training for a marathon in London. Hearing from people how they have been inspired by these videos, and that they have had such a huge impact, is incredibly rewarding, and gives the videos a real purpose.

It was when I transitioned to a plant-based way of eating that my love of cooking really took off

MY HEALTH JOURNEY

When I was younger, I never cooked at all. My grandma and mum have always been good cooks, but I was never interested. I actually remember once telling them I would never cook, and that I'd just have to find a partner, when I was older, who could do it for me. Whenever I went to my grandparents' house after school, my grandma would sit me on the stool in the kitchen, while she made dinner. I'd sit and chat with her, catching up on each other's days, and didn't realize that I was subconsciously learning what she was doing—she now admits to doing this for that exact purpose! For some reason, cooking seemed a waste of time and boring, but then a few years ago, I realized how important it was to prepare nutritious, homemade meals, using fresh ingredients, and what an impact it would have on my overall well-being.

I want to inspire others to feel good by cooking food that nourishes the body

Around the time that I started to look into a healthier way of living, a couple of people in my life were diagnosed with serious illnesses, one of whom didn't make it. Fortunately for me, it wasn't an immediate family member, but the pain and hurt I saw in their relatives made me realize just how fragile life is. It made me question the food we have become accustomed to eating now—fast and processed, pumped full of sugar, salt, additives, and all kinds of chemicals that are difficult to digest (mentally and physically). It made me wonder what sort of an effect these foods have on our bodies. I started researching this, and I couldn't believe how detrimental it can be to your health to eat this way. I decided to cut out processed foods and started to cook my own meals at home, instead of buying prepared meals, which was great, but I was still eating meat, fish, dairy, and eggs. However, while doing my research, the plant-based way of eating seemed to be a recurring topic.

Like many others, I had hugely misinterpreted eating a plant-based diet as being restricted to bland salads lacking in flavor or substance. Unfortunately, the word "vegan" has a stigma attached to it. People picture "vegans" as pale, ill, and incredibly preachy about the way they eat. Some people may also think it's virtually impossible to eat a vegan diet, because they will run out of things to eat, or the food simply won't taste as good. However, I decided to look into it more, and noticed how appealing plant-based eating sounded. I'm a pretty open-minded person, and love discovering new things, asking hundreds of questions of interesting people, and finding out why they have made certain choices in life.

The more research I did, the more fascinating it was to hear about how much of a positive impact plant-based eating was having on people around the world, from supposedly curing illnesses to simply having more energy. I knew I couldn't come to my own decision until I tried it myself, so that's when I cut out all meat, fish, dairy, and eggs from my diet overnight, to see how it made me feel.

I had no idea how long I would eat this way, because I decided to listen to my body, rather than limiting myself to a set time period. After only a couple of weeks of eating plant-based food, I couldn't believe how different I felt. I had so much more energy, my skin looked clearer and brighter than ever, my hair and nails were growing at the speed of light, and I felt happier and more positive. Since that day, more than two years ago, I haven't looked back, which is why I wanted to create this book.

THE PLANT-BASED LIFESTYLE

This way of eating is all about embracing a lifestyle that may be quite different from what you're used to. I call this lifestyle plant-based, not vegan, because vegan refers to a diet and lifestyle that eliminates all animal products altogether—including honey—while a plant-based diet eliminates food products that come from animals, but can include honey, which I do eat occasionally, provided it's locally and ethically sourced.

I never count calories. I think it's far more important to eat when you're hungry, stop eating when you're full, and try to eat an abundance of whole foods

I chose to make a dramatic change in the way I ate overnight, but if I were to do it again, I would take it step by step, to make it easier to adjust to all the changes. The prospect of a plant-based diet can seem daunting at first, because you focus on the things you have to cut out, rather than on the amazing things that you'll be introducing. So take small steps for a few weeks until you reach a point where you feel really happy. You don't have to go completely plant-based. I believe the way you eat is subjective, because only you know what truly works for your own body. This way of eating suits me well, but it won't appeal to everyone, so try it, listen to your body, and find the right balance. The main thing is to avoid processed foods and eat more fresh produce whenever you can.

The main motivator for me is knowing that I'm looking after myself, keeping myself healthy, and respecting my body. One thing I should also mention is that I honestly couldn't tell you what my daily caloric intake is, because I'm just not interested. For me, eating well isn't about restricting myself to a specific caloric intake. For instance, nuts, avocados, and coconuts are high in calories, but their amazing health benefits outweigh the high calories.

MY INSPIRATION

Thanks to my flexible job on YouTube, I'm lucky to have traveled to many different countries, over the past few years, and experienced various cultures and kinds of food. Many of my recipes have been inspired by the meals I have eaten while traveling, but they are created here with my own touch. I've adapted these authentic cooking methods to make the recipes easy and accessible, and always I use fresh ingredients, keeping health at the forefront of my mind.

My first experience of Asia was on a trip to Bali in 2015. The people were so friendly, happy, and accommodating—I learned a lot about the food there, particularly when one local invited me into her home and talked me through her typical daily meals. The Balinese really value the importance of eating well to nurture themselves for overall health, well-being, and spirituality. A local told me how when she gets sick she often heals herself, first through food and herbs, before going to a conventional doctor. I, too, try to avoid over-the-counter medication wherever I can. Since eating this way, I have rarely become ill, but when I feel a cold or flu coming on, I nourish myself with natural food and spices, such as ginger, oranges, and turmeric.

Traveling has opened my eyes to different ingredients and encouraged me not to be scared of experimenting with food. The people whom I've met all over the world have really cemented my views on health and well-being, but there are also people online whom I have never met, but who have had a big impact on my views, including Brendan Brazier, who created the Vega brand, and Matt Frazier, of the No Meat Athlete blog, whose podcasts I listen to while running.

CHANGING THE WAY YOU EAT

The hardest thing about changing the way you eat is most definitely the social aspect. Your friends and family may not approve of your eating healthier at first, which sounds crazy, right? Being healthy has a stigma attached to it—people often think those who eat healthily are obsessive and self-obsessed. But this isn't always the case. When I first gave up meat, eggs, and dairy, many people were actually worried about my health, which baffled me, because I was doing it for the opposite reason.

Another obstacle to overcome, when you change the way you eat, is finding places to eat out. Although many people have certain dietary requirements, it can still be tricky to find a place that has something suitable on the menu. However, to this day, I have never had to leave a cafe or restaurant because they had nothing for me. I used to be embarrassed explaining to restaurant staff that I ate a plant-based diet, especially with people that I didn't know too well, but now I have realized that if you don't say anything, you're just going to be stuck with the one thing that's vegan on the menu—most likely a plain side salad. Eating this way is a positive, and nothing to be embarrassed by. You'd be surprised by how many people are interested and may be inspired.

Preparation is key. In the evenings, I cook more than I will eat, so that I have plenty of leftovers for lunch the next day—and food often tastes even better the next day, because the flavors intensify overnight. Weekends are a great opportunity to make healthy snacks, such as energy balls (see page 168) for the week ahead. I'm such a grazer, I like to have my handbag well-stocked with healthy snacks and drinks.

An important aspect of any change in the way you eat is to be sure that you will not be lacking any vital vitamins and minerals. I've made sure that the recipes in *Eat Smart* include foods that are naturally high in vitamins and minerals, but on a plant-based diet, the vitamins and minerals you may need to be more aware of are vitamin B12, calcium, iron, and vitamin D, as well as omega-3 and protein.

There are so many natural plant-based sources of protein, such as peas, nuts, black beans, lentils, and quinoa. I also occasionally add a vegan protein powder to my smoothies.

Calcium can be easily obtained from sources such as kale, chickpeas, and black strap molasses, and you can get sufficient amounts of iron through whole grains, lentils, chickpeas, and, once again, blackstrap molasses. To get a healthy amount of omega-3, include walnuts, chia seeds, and flaxseed in your diet. You can also find non-dairy milks that are fortified with certain vitamins, too.

The two supplements that I take are B12 and vitamin D. Vitamin D can be gained purely from exposure to sunlight, but unfortunately that's not so common in the UK! You can also get vitamin D from mushrooms, but they have to be U V treated, and it can be hard to know that for sure. A lack of vitamin B12 can cause serious health problems, so it's one to be aware of. Even though B12 itself is a vegan product, it can be hard to get by eating only plant-based food. The best way to get B12 is to take a supplement—either as a capsule, tongue spray, injection, or sublingual tablets. Sublingual tablets are small and sweet-tasting and can be placed under your tongue until they dissolve—this is the most effective way of getting B12 into your body, because it doesn't have to go through the digestive system.

Fitting healthy eating into a busy lifestyle isn't as hard as you think

EXERCISE

At school I was never one of the naturally sporty kids, but I did enjoy a select few sports, such as cross-country running. For any other sports, I would come up with a million and one excuses to get out of them. Since becoming aware of the importance of eating well, I have also taken up exercising; the two go hand in hand. Fortunately, I now really enjoy working out and keeping fit. I love that feeling you have for the rest of the day after exercise.

I tend to work out three to five times a week, and always mix up the sessions. My favorite workout is running, because it gets your heart rate up, which is obviously the best thing for your cardiovascular health. I only run outdoors, rather than in a gym, because I find it more mentally stimulating, meaning I can run further, and have got to know London better.

I also love strength training, using weights or my own body weight to tone up. I find it motivating to see the changes in my body, and notice how much stronger I feel. I do yoga once a week to stretch my muscles, especially as I do so much running, which has quite a high impact on the joints and muscles. It's important to include a lower-intensity workout if you're exercising a lot, and yoga is my favorite choice for the downtime it gives me to relax and clear my mind.

I'm an early bird and have more energy at the start of the day, so I have always preferred to get active in the morning. If you need a little motivation to go to the gym in the morning, here's a tip: lay out your gym shoes and workout clothes the night before, and make one of my overnight breakfasts, so you can throw on your gear and grab something to eat as soon as you wake up, and get straight to the gym without even thinking about it!

Many people think that eating plant-based foods won't provide as much energy or muscle growth as a standard diet, but actually it is quite the opposite. I've never felt more energetic or fitter, and it has fueled me to run the London Marathon, which is a staggering 26.2 miles. Running the marathon was not something I'd thought about doing before, but when I was approached by a charity to run it for them, of course I took up the opportunity. I am convinced that had I not been eating the way I do now, I wouldn't have enjoyed it as much, and most definitely would have struggled.

A lot of what I eat in a day depends on how much energy I use, so if I'm doing an intense workout, I'll focus on getting more carbohydrates. On rest days, when I don't exercise, I lower my intake of carbs, because my body just doesn't need the extra energy. And whenever I crave something filling and satisfying, I opt for something higher in fat, like almond butter.

Exercise makes me feel great physically and psychologically, and sets me up for the rest of the day, feeling positive, upbeat, and generally happier

SUPERFOODS

"Superfood" is the name given to nutrient-dense foods that contain lots of vitamins, minerals, and antioxidants. Although they don't cancel out an unhealthy diet, they can add an extra health boost. I am a huge advocate of superfoods and think they are a great addition to any diet.

In recent years, the food industry has raised the prices of many superfood supplements and powders, which are now a multi-billion-dollar industry, so it can be expensive and also confusing to know which superfoods are worth the money. You may find you are already eating superfoods in everyday ingredients, such as fresh fruit.

I eat the sort of everyday superfoods that can be found in any store, at any time, but I also love to use some of the more unusual ones. Discovering new superfoods can be fun because you get to experiment with ingredients and find out which ones work well together, as they all have different flavors. Some have a caramel taste, while others may not taste so great, and need to be disguised in a fruity smoothie. It's true that superfoods have gained a reputation in the media, and now have the price tag to show for it, but it's all about trying different ones and finding out which work best for you.

Superfoods don't necessarily have to be expensive powders from health food stores; you may find you are already eating them

EVERYDAY SUPERFOODS

Blueberries	High in fiber, vitamin C, and K, blueberries contain a high amount of antioxidants. Antioxidants have been shown to help accelerate muscle recovery and reduce inflammation, making them a great post-workout snack. I add a handful to oatmeal, granola, or smoothies.
Kale	A very nutritious and versatile food, kale is high in fiber, vitamin A, C, and K, and provides a wealth of benefits, including healthy skin and a strengthened immune system.
Sweet Potato	These are more nutrient-dense than white potatoes, taste better, and have a lower glycemic index, meaning blood sugar levels will increase more gradually.
Garlic	For centuries, garlic has been used as a natural remedy all around the world, because it acts as a natural antibiotic, fighting off viral and bacterial infections, and contains strong immune-boosting properties that help to battle cold and flu symptoms.
Nuts	I include a lot of different nuts in my recipes, because they are packed with protein, fiber, and essential fats. You can eat a handful-sized portion as a snack, or you can sprinkle them over salads for texture. I have a few favorites, each with their own health benefits.
Walnuts	These are famous as some of the most super of all superfood nuts, because they contain high levels of antioxidants and healthy fats, which help keep your heart, skin, and hair healthy.
Almonds	Almonds are a good source of healthy fats, which help keep cholesterol levels low. They are also high in vitamin E and magnesium. They're great for anyone who is avoiding dairy, as they are rich in calcium, which is great for bone density.

These are so beneficial that some people actually eat 1 or 2 a day, as you might take a regular vitamin. More than any other food, Brazil nuts contain selenium, a mineral high in antioxidants that may help brain function, promote a healthy thyroid, and keep hair and nails healthy.

Brazil Nuts

EXOTIC SUPERFOODS

Packed with fiber and protein, omega-3s, and healthy fats vital for brain health. Mixed with water, they swell and can be used as an egg replacer. I love to add them to smoothies, too.

Chia Seeds

Another great substitute for eggs in baking, but use the milled version, not whole seeds, for a more discrete flavor and texture. High in protein, fiber, omega-3s, and minerals and vitamins, such as magnesium and iron.

Flaxseeds (Linseeds)

Milled from fruit grown in Africa on the baobab tree, it's incredibly high in antioxidants, nutrients, and minerals, with a sherbet citrus taste. Rich in vitamin C, it provides a natural energy boost, so add a tablespoon to smoothies.

Baobab Powder

Known for centuries to be a natural aphrodisiac, maca is believed to boost energy levels, balance hormones, and improve mood, making it a great option for anyone who suffers from depression, anxiety, or mood disorders.

Maca Powder

Cacao is raw, unprocessed chocolate from the cacao bean, and it contains high levels of antioxidants. Do not confuse it with cocoa, which is processed and less nutritious. Research shows that cacao helps improve circulation, cardiovascular health, and mood, and contains magnesium, calcium, zinc, and iron.

Raw Cacao Powder and Nibs

Matcha	This powdered green tea has been used for thousands of years in Japan. Matcha is believed to speed up metabolism, is packed with antioxidants and gives you an energy boost—a great replacement for coffee.
Spirulina Powder	An excellent source of protein, which helps to build and strengthen muscles, spirulina has all the essential amino acids. This alga contains powerful antioxidants and is rich in vitamins, as well as vital minerals, particularly B vitamins.
Açaí Powder	A great superfood, açaí has a delicious berry taste and is rich in antioxidants. I love to use it in smoothies, because it provides an instant hit of energy, as well as vital minerals and vitamins.

HERBS

Basil	I use this tasty herb mainly in Italian recipes, such as pesto, or in salads, and also to garnish pasta dishes. Basil is also believed to ease stomach problems.
Cilantro	This herb goes especially well with spicy Mexican and Indian dishes. It can be used fresh, or you can use the powder from the coriander seeds. Both have a distinct flavor and contain many vitamins, including vitamins A, C, and K.
Mint	A very versatile herb that goes well in many sweet dishes, as well as salads and refreshing, summery drinks. Mint has been used for thousands of years for its medicinal properties, notably for soothing stomach aches and pains.

This is an herb with delicate flavors that I find works well in fresh salads. It is rich in vital vitamins, antioxidants, and minerals that help reduce the risk of diseases.

Parsley

I love to roast vegetables in fresh rosemary. The aroma it creates always reminds me of Christmas! Besides being one of the most flavorful herbs, it is also known for boosting memory and mood.

Rosemary

This is one of those herbs that seems to go with everything, but I particularly like pairing it with bananas in sweet recipes, such as my oat bars (see page 221). The essential oils in thyme have also been shown to help cure bacterial infections.

Thyme

I use this herb in its dried form for lots of recipes; try it in my Squashetti + "Meatballs" (see page 104) and Mexican Chili Bowl (see page 99).

Oregano

You can easily find dried mixed herbs in the supermarket. They're great to have on hand, to add a hit of flavor to any dish.

Mixed Herbs

SPICES

Cayenne Pepper	I use the dried, ground version of this hot red chili pepper to add a hit of spiciness. Cayenne is rich in antioxidants and is believed to improve circulation.
Chili Powder	Simply dried and ground chilies—a quick, easy way to spice up your meals when you don't have any fresh chilis.
Cinnamon	I use ground cinnamon in many of my recipes, mainly because I love the taste, but also because it is rich in antioxidants, and it is believed to improve metabolism and reduce inflammation.
Cumin	I use ground cumin, or whole seeds, in many recipes for its nutty, earthy taste. Its essential oils also help promote healthy digestion.
Ginger	I use ground ginger when I don't want the bulkiness and moisture of fresh ginger, but still want the flavor.
Paprika	There are many types available, ranging from sweet to smoky and spicy. I choose regular or smoked paprika, rather than spicy; if I want some heat, I'll add a pinch of cayenne pepper. Paprika is high in vitamin C, which helps keep skin healthy.
Turmeric	This adds a vibrant yellow color to dishes. Turmeric has been used for hundreds of years as an anti-inflammatory. In fact, I used it in a salve, recently, to cure an infected finger.
Pure Vanilla Extract or Powder	A great addition to any sweet recipe, particularly cakes and cookies. Nothing beats the flavor of the seeds, straight from the pod, but they can be expensive. I usually use powder, ground beans, or pure extract.

STAPLES

One of the biggest barriers people find to changing the way they eat is the myth that healthy recipes need expensive, obscure ingredients. While eating healthily can be expensive, if you're constantly buying the superfood of the moment, it doesn't have to break the bank. Once you stock up with staple ingredients that'll keep for a long time, you'll only need to buy fresh fruit and vegetables. When I changed the way I ate, I noticed how much money I was saving by not buying meat, seafood, and dairy.

I bought most of the ingredients in this book from the little supermarket near me. So don't worry about needing to hunt these down—most supermarkets have a healthy or "free-from" aisle containing everything from quinoa and bulgar wheat to dairy-free milk and yogurt. I do like to go to health food stores occasionally, though, because the quality can be better, and they have my favorite brands.

There are some ingredients here that you might not have cooked with before, such as black rice, but they are easy to find and surprisingly simple to use. Once you've tried them a few times, I guarantee they will become favorite staples.

Occasionally I use ingredients, such as coconut sugar, which may be harder to find in smaller supermarkets. So rather than traipsing around stores, order them online to find the best deal, and perhaps buy in bulk to save money, too.

Most of my recipes are made with fresh, wholesome ingredients that can be found in your local supermarket

PANTRY STAPLES

I use whole black peppercorns in a grinder.	Black Pepper
This is less processed and refined than table salt. It is also higher in minerals, such as boron, zinc, and phosphorus, needed for healthy hair, nails, skin, and thyroid function. I always taste food before seasoning it, and try to use as little salt as possible.	Pink Himalayan Salt
This is natural, unrefined, and contains many essential mineral elements. If you don't have pink Himalayan salt, use this instead.	Sea Salt
This oil is highly resistant to oxidation at high heat levels, so it is ideal for cooking. Coconut oil is said to have remarkable health benefits, and I find it's lovely to cook with because it adds a wonderful, subtle flavor to all kinds of dishes.	Raw Unrefined Coconut Oil
Delicious as a dressing on salads or raw pestos. I tend to cook with coconut oil and use extra-virgin olive oil in cold, raw dishes.	Extra-virgin Olive Oil
This is my non-dairy milk of choice; I love the taste, it goes well with hot and cold cereal, and helps thicken dishes. Rice milk and coconut milk are delicious alternatives.	Unsweetened Almond Milk
I buy natural and organic almond butter, without added sugar or salt, and use it in desserts, in smoothies for a protein kick, or on crackers as an afternoon snack.	Almond Butter
I always make sure I am well stocked with oats. I buy rolled, gluten-free oats. I also grind them into a flour and bake with it.	Oats
My grain of choice; it is so versatile and a complete protein. I use it instead of white rice or pasta, cold and mixed into salads, or in stews. I've also made a granola with it (see page 46).	Quinoa
I always use the canned, full-fat version so that it's as close to its natural form as possible. It's perfect for adding creaminess to soups, curries, and desserts.	Coconut Milk

Maple Syrup	This is a 100% natural and pure sweetener straight from the maple tree, retaining many of its minerals and antioxidants. It has a lovely, distinctive flavor that adds depth to baked goods. Use pure versions, rather than maple-flavored syrups.
Coconut Sugar (or Palm Sugar)	A great replacement for white sugar. Although it is more expensive, a little goes a long way, so it lasts longer. It offers more nutrients and minerals and has a lower glycemic index than refined sugars.
Buckwheat Flour	I avoid using all-purpose white flour because it's so heavily processed and contains few nutritional benefits. Buckwheat flour can be used for pancakes, muffins, and other baked goods.
Spelt Flour	A great alternative to all-purpose flour; it contains many more nutrients than white flour and is high in protein and fiber.
Dates	With their delicious caramel flavor, many minerals, vitamins, and high fiber content, dates are so versatile. I buy Medjool dates, because they tend to be plump and moist.
Nuts	Almonds and cashews are my favorites because they contain a high level of protein and nutrients. Raw, unsalted nuts, without oil, are the most nutritious.
Brown Rice	This type of rice is slower to digest then white rice and releases energy slowly; it is also high in fiber and protein.
Apple Cider Vinegar	This tastes especially good in salad dressings. It has many health benefits and is believed to significantly help digestion. Surprisingly, it's also good as a raising agent in baking.
Nutritional Yeast	Despite the off-putting name, this has a cheesy flavor that can be used as a Parmesan substitute. Get the kind that says it's fortified with B12. It's also gluten-free, high in fiber and protein, and contains folic acid.

FRESH STAPLES

Research shows that garlic has many health benefits, including anti-inflammatory, antiviral, and antibacterial properties. For me, nothing beats a strong garlic kick, so I add it to many of my recipes.

Garlic

I use fresh ginger a lot. It contains many minerals and vitamins and has been used for millennia to calm stomach issues.

Ginger

These citrus fruits have amazing antioxidant properties. Add them to juices, salads, or even curries to reap their health benefits.

Lemons and Limes

I always have these around to add to my pre-workout morning smoothies for sweetness and to create a thick, creamy texture. This potassium-rich fruit is high in carbs, making you feel fuller for longer, slowly releasing energy into the body. I wait until they are ripe with brown spots before I use them, and if they get over-ripe, I freeze them, peeled and cut into chunks, to use another time, usually in my Açaí Bowl (see page 37).

Bananas

These are always in my fridge. I love the taste, and they are also very high in antioxidants. I often scatter them over hot cereal or granola.

Blueberries

These are less starchy and richer in nutrients than white potatoes. They also taste incredibly delicious, so I eat them about three times a week, sometimes more!

Sweet Potatoes

Rich in many vitamins and minerals, particularly iron. A great way to make the most of this is to add a handful of raw leaves to a smoothie, exploiting their mild taste.

Spinach

Of course, this classic "superfood" vegetable is one of my staples. I like to add it to smoothies and juices for an extra health kick. I also like to steam kale as a side dish at dinner, or eat it for lunch with a squeeze of fresh lemon.

Kale

BASIC EQUIPMENT

Blender	A blender is a great addition to any kitchen. I use mine to make my smoothies and also to make pesto, crush nuts, and grind oats into flour.
Juicer	For smooth juices, use a juicer that extracts the pulp. Prices vary hugely, but you can buy one for as little as $30.00.
Food Processor	Not an absolute necessity, but the more you get into cooking the more you may find it makes life a lot easier. I love my food processor for making anything from cake batters and burger mixtures to creamy cashew cheese and pestos. Again, prices vary, but you can get a cheap one that does a good job.
Spiralizer	I'm a big fan of spiralizing vegetables—turning them into long noodle-like shapes—as a great alternative to pasta, or to make salads more exciting. They're inexpensive, too.
Measuring Cups	These are probably the most used and loved pieces of equipment in my kitchen. I use measuring cups instead of scales, as I find them quicker and more convenient to use. You can find them almost anywhere for a couple of dollars.
Measuring Spoons	I like the ease and precision of using these, but you can also just use your regular teaspoons and tablespoons, as long as you use them consistently for measuring ingredients.
Garlic Mincer	I find this so useful because it takes a fraction of the amount of time it takes to chop garlic by hand, and also prevents your fingers from smelling like garlic. You can find these in most grocery stores.
Vegetable Peeler	A pretty obvious one, but a staple in my kitchen nonetheless.

If you don't want to fork over the dough for a food processor, I would recommend purchasing a mortar and pestle to crush nuts and seeds.	Mortar and Pestle
To get the most nutrients from your vegetables, steam rather than boil them. You can buy electric steamers, but I have always used a three-tiered stainless-steel steamer that you can use on the stove, for a fraction of the price.	Steamer
It is important to get some good-quality nonstick pans. Although they're slightly more expensive, they last longer, therefore justifying the price, in my opinion.	Nonstick Pans
I have two basic baking pans 10" x 14" and 11" x 17" and two roasting pans 10½" x 15½" and 12½" x 17½".	Roasting and Baking Pans
I use an 8-inch, springform cake pan—so I can unclip the sides. It also has a loose bottom to release the cake easily.	Cake Pan
I have a couple of different-sized loaf pans, but usually I use a 9 x 5-inch pan.	Loaf Pan
I use a 9-inch enamel pie pan.	Pie Pan

...at to dry,

...ed glass jar.

...jar to release any trapped

...direct sunlight for 3–4 weeks to let
...s infuse. It will take at least 10 days for
...vors to develop and about 3–4 weeks for
...um flavor. If the flavor is too strong, you can
...e it by adding additional "base" vinegar, or if it
...too weak, let it infuse longer.

Once the desired flavor is reached, strain vinegar
...through cheesecloth into non-metallic bowl or jug
...card the solids.

...ered vinegar into an airtight bottle for
...a few sprigs of fresh herbs can be
...before sealing. Store in a cool,

...ons

Breakfast

01

I discovered smoothie bowls in L.A., at a quirky cafe called Juice Generation, and the best I've ever tasted were in Bali. They were a revelation to me and since then I've made my own versions, trying out different combinations of fruit and superfoods.

AÇAÍ

Serves 2

Ingredients

3 frozen bananas, peeled
¼ cup (25g) fresh or
    frozen blueberries,
    raspberries, and blackberries
½ cup (125ml) unsweetened
    almond milk
2 tbsp açaí powder
2 tbsp maca powder (optional)

SUPERFOOD CHOCOLATE

Serves 2

Ingredients

3 frozen bananas, peeled, chopped
1 tbsp raw cacao powder
1 tbsp chia seeds
1 tbsp lucuma powder (optional)
½ cup (125ml) unsweetened
    almond milk

TROPICAL

Serves 2

Ingredients

a large handful of spinach
½ cup (100g) frozen mango chunks
½ cup (100g) frozen pineapple chunks
¼ cucumber
¼ cup (60ml) coconut water,
    plus extra if needed
2 ice cubes
1 tsp baobab powder (optional)
1 tsp spirulina (optional)

1. Simply place all the ingredients in a blender (make sure your blender can work with frozen fruit).

2. Blend until creamy and smooth, adding extra almond milk or coconut water, if needed.

3. Serve in bowls, decorated with toppings of your choice.

Tip ... When bananas get overripe, peel and roughly chop them, place them in a freezer bag, and freeze the bananas so you have them to make smoothie bowls.

Topping ideas ...
Sliced bananas
Fresh berries
Dried mulberries
Goji berries
Sunflower seeds
Pumpkin seeds
Chia seeds
Hemp seeds
Coconut flakes
Almond butter
Homemade granola (see page 46)

OATMEAL—3 WAYS

I'm a huge fan of oatmeal—it's one of the best breakfasts, providing so much energy that it usually keeps me going until lunch. I like experimenting with different flavors. These recipes are inspired by some favorite desserts—and who doesn't want to eat dessert for breakfast, when it it's good for you?

BANANA BREAD

Serves 2

Ingredients

1 cup (100g) rolled oats
1 cup (250ml) unsweetened
   almond milk
1 ripe banana, peeled
¼ cup (30g) raisins
1 tsp ground cinnamon
¼ tsp ground nutmeg
1 tsp maca powder (optional)

1. Place the oats, almond milk, and 1 cup (250ml) water into a small saucepan and place it over medium-low heat.

2. Thinly slice and stir in half the banana with the raisins, cinnamon, nutmeg, and maca powder, if using. Cook, stirring regularly, for 5–7 minutes, or until thick and creamy and the oats have absorbed all the liquid.

3. Thinly slice the remaining banana and serve the oatmeal topped with the banana slices and any other toppings you like.

🥣 Serving ideas ...
A teaspoon of my homemade Strawberry Chia Jam (see page 56).

CARROT CAKE

Serves 2

Ingredients

1 cup (100g) rolled oats
1 cup (250ml) unsweetened
   almond milk
1 carrot, peeled and grated
1 tbsp date syrup or maple syrup
¼ tsp each of ground cinnamon,
   ground nutmeg, and
   ground ginger
¼ (30g) cup raisins

1. Put the oats, almond milk, and 1 cup (250ml) water into a small saucepan and place it over medium heat.

2. Stir in most of the carrot, along with the syrup, cinnamon, nutmeg, ginger, and raisins. Cook, stirring regularly, for 5–7 minutes, or until thick and creamy.

3. Sprinkle the remaining carrot and any other toppings you like over the oatmeal and serve.

🥣 Serving ideas ...
A small handful of chopped, unsalted, raw walnuts.

CHERRY BAKE

Serves 2

Ingredients

1 cup (100g) rolled oats
1 cup (250ml) unsweetened almond milk
4 fresh cherries, pitted
1 tbsp almond butter
1 tbsp ground almonds
1 tsp organic vanilla extract
1 tbsp maple syrup

Serving ideas ...
A small handful of chopped almonds.
Fresh cherries, pitted, and halved.

1. Put the oats, almond milk, and 1 cup (250ml) water into a small saucepan and set it over medium heat.

2. Roughly chop the cherries and stir them into the saucepan with the almond butter, ground almonds, vanilla extract, and maple syrup. Cook for 5–6 minutes, stirring regularly, or until thick and creamy.

SMOOTH BANANA + BLUEBERRY OATMEAL

Serves 2

I love this banana-flavored oatmeal, which is easily made by blending all the ingredients until they are super smooth. The whole blueberries, once heated, burst and provide a delicious pop of flavor.

Ingredients

2 ripe bananas, peeled
1 cup (100g) rolled oats
2 cups (500ml)
    unsweetened
    almond milk
1 tsp ground cinnamon
1 cup (100g)
    blueberries

1. Blend 1½ bananas with the oats, almond milk, and cinnamon until smooth.

2. Pour the banana mixture into a small saucepan and stir in the blueberries.

3. Place the mixture in a small saucepan and cook it over low heat for 5–6 minutes, stirring regularly, until the oatmeal is thick and creamy.

4. Slice the remaining half of the banana and serve it on top of the oatmeal with any other toppings you might like.

Topping ideas ...
Almond butter
Fresh blueberries
Pumpkin seeds

PEAR QUINOA PORRIDGE

Serves 2

Quinoa is now widely known as a superfood grain. It's a complete protein, which means it contains all nine of the amino acids that we need, which is rare for a plant-based food. I wanted to use it to create a breakfast, and, as I'm a porridge fanatic, I came up with this warming, subtly sweet dish, served with pear for a lovely fresh taste.

Ingredients

½ cup (100g) quinoa, rinsed
1½ cups (375ml) unsweetened almond milk, plus extra (optional)
2 ripe pears, cored
juice of ½ lemon
1 tsp ground cinnamon
1 tsp vanilla powder or 2 tsp organic vanilla extract
a handful of chopped, unsalted, raw walnuts, to serve
maple syrup (optional), to serve

1. Place the quinoa in a saucepan with the almond milk and ½ cup (125ml) of water, and cook over medium–high heat. Bring to a boil, then turn the heat down to low and simmer for 15 minutes, stirring occasionally, until the liquid has been absorbed and the quinoa is cooked. Add extra almond milk, if needed.

2. Thinly slice a quarter of one of the pears and set it aside. Chop the rest of that pear and the remaining pears into small chunks and stir them into the cooked quinoa with the lemon juice, cinnamon, and vanilla.

3. Serve the quinoa with the chopped walnuts and the sliced pear. If you would like something a little sweeter, drizzle some maple syrup over the top.

●━● Tip ... To help reduce the earthy taste quinoa sometimes has, simply cook off the moisture in a dry pan over low heat for a few seconds. Shake the pan frequently to keep the quinoa from burning.

OVERNIGHT BREAKFAST JARS—3 WAYS

If you often find yourself skipping breakfast in the mornings, why not make an overnight breakfast jar? I make these in the evening, and overnight the oats plump up and the flavors intensify. In the morning I can just grab one and go!

APPLE + BLUEBERRY

Serves 1

Ingredients

creamy oat layer
½ apple, cored and grated
½ cup (50g) rolled oats
½ cup (125ml) unsweetened
    almond milk
½ tsp ground cinnamon

blueberry layer
1 tbsp chia seeds
½ cup (50g) blueberries
¾-inch piece of fresh ginger,
    peeled and finely grated
2 tsp açaí powder (optional)
a handful of blueberries, to serve
a handful of chopped unsalted,
    raw macadamia nuts, to serve

1. Mix together the apple, oats, almond milk, and cinnamon and set aside.

2. Mix the chia seeds with 5 tablespoons of water in a bowl. Mash the blueberries with a fork and add to the chia with the ginger and açaí powder, if using.

3. Spoon half the oat mixture into a 2-cup jar and layer it with half the blueberry mixture. Repeat until both mixtures are used up.

4. Seal the jar with a lid and keep it in the fridge overnight. By the morning, it'll be ready to eat. Sprinkle over the toppings and dig in.

STRAWBERRIES + "CREAM"

Serves 1

Ingredients

strawberry layer
6 strawberries, hulled

creamy oat layer
½ ripe banana, peeled
½ cup (50g) rolled oats
½ cup (125ml) unsweetened
    almond milk
¼ x 14-oz (400-g) can coconut milk
¼ tsp vanilla powder or ½ tsp
    organic vanilla extract

1. Thinly slice the strawberries and mash the banana with the back of a fork.

2. Mix the mashed banana in a bowl with the remaining ingredients, except the strawberries.

3. Spoon a third of the creamy banana oat mixture into a 2-cup jar. Layer the jar with a few of the sliced strawberries and add another layer of the oat mixture. Repeat until used up.

4. Seal the jar with a lid and keep it in the fridge overnight. By morning, the oats will have thickened up, ready for you to dig in.

→● Tip ... Freeze the leftover banana to make a smoothie bowl another time.

PINK BERRY

Serves 1

Ingredients

1 cup (125g) raspberries
1 heaping tsp açaí powder (optional)
1 cup (250ml) unsweetened
 almond milk
½ cup (50g) rolled oats
3 tbsp chia seeds
1 tbsp goji berries
a small handful of unsalted raw
 pistachios, to serve

1. Blend together the fresh berries, açaí powder, if using, and almond milk until smooth.

2. Pour the mixture into a 2-cup jar and stir in the oats, chia seeds, and goji berries. Refrigerate overnight in a tightly sealed jar.

3. In the morning, sprinkle the oat mixture with the pistachios and dig in.

Breakfast

GRANOLA

I make this over the weekend and store it in an airtight container—so it is ready to go at all times. It will last a few weeks, but it's so addictive it's usually gone before that! My cacao and coconut version of granola makes me feel like a kid with chocolaty cereal. And yes, you get the same choco milk effect!

CACAO + COCONUT

Makes 16 servings

Ingredients

4 tbsp coconut oil
4 tbsp maple syrup
4 tbsp unsweetened almond milk
¼ cup (30g) raw cacao powder
3 cups (300g) rolled oats
½ cup (30g) coconut flakes
½ cup (100g) quinoa, rinsed
¼ cup (25g) dried unsweetened coconut
¼ cup (30g) raw cacao nibs

1. Preheat the oven to 325°F/170°C.

2. Heat the coconut oil in a small saucepan over low heat until it melts, then stir in the maple syrup, almond milk, and cacao powder and remove from the heat.

3. Stir together the oats, coconut flakes, quinoa, dried unsweetened coconut, and cacao nibs. Pour the wet mixture into a bowl and stir until everything is fully coated.

4. Pour the mixture onto a baking pan and gently press the mixture down with the back of a wooden spoon.

5. Bake the granola in the oven for 30 minutes, stirring occasionally, then remove it from the oven and allow it to cool.

MIXED FRUIT + NUT

Makes 16 servings

Ingredients

4 tbsp coconut oil
½ cup (125ml) maple syrup
2 cups (200g) rolled oats
1 cup (160g) unsalted raw almonds
1 cup (100g) unsalted raw pecans
½ cup (60g) pumpkin seeds
½ cup (30g) coconut flakes
1 cup (120g) chopped dried fruit, such as unsulphured apricots, Medjool dates, figs, raisins, and prunes

1. Preheat the oven to 325°F/170°C. Heat the coconut oil in a small saucepan over low heat until it melts, then stir in the maple syrup and remove from the heat.

2. Stir together the oats, almonds, pecans, and pumpkin seeds.

3. Pour the melted coconut oil and maple syrup mixture into a bowl and stir to fully coat. Then pour the mixture onto a baking pan and press it down with a wooden spoon.

4. Bake the granola in the oven for 30 minutes, stirring occasionally. Add the coconut flakes after 15 minutes. Remove the granola from the oven and allow it to cool. Stir in the dried fruit and store in an airtight container.

MUESLI

Makes 12 servings

As a serial cereal eater, this is my go-to breakfast during the week. Muesli is one of those things you often just buy ready-made, but it's so easy to throw together. Why not make it over the weekend and set yourself up with a wholesome breakfast for the next few mornings?

Ingredients

1 cup (100g) rolled oats
1 cup (30g) puffed
   brown rice
1 cup (100g) rye flakes
   or barley flakes
½ cup (50g)
   sliced almonds
½ cup (50g)
   goji berries
½ cup (30g)
   coconut flakes
¼ cup (30g) dried
   cranberries
   or golden raisins
¼ cup (30g)
   sunflower seeds
½ tsp ground
   cinnamon

1. Place all the ingredients in a large bowl, mix them together, and store the muesli in an airtight container. That's it!

🥣 Serving ideas ...

Almond milk and a handful of mixed fresh berries.

BIRCHER MUESLI

Serves 2

In the summer, I crave a refreshing, light breakfast. This muesli is perfect; you only need to take it out of the fridge in the morning, grab a spoon, and tuck in. My traditional Swiss recipe for Bircher Muesli uses only natural sugars from the fruit and no dairy products. Try mixing it up with different toppings!

Ingredients

1 red apple
1 tbsp lemon juice
½ tsp ground
  cinnamon
¼ cup (40g) unsalted
  raw almonds
1 cup (100g)
  rolled oats
¼ cup (30g) raisins
1 heaping tbsp golden
  flaxseed
1 heaping tbsp
  sunflower seeds
2 cups (500ml)
  unsweetened
  almond or
  rice milk

1. Core the apple and grate it into a large bowl, then add the lemon juice and cinnamon, and mix together.

2. Grind the almonds into small pieces, using a mortar and pestle or a food processor. Add the almonds to the bowl with the remaining ingredients and mix well.

3. Cover the bowl with plastic wrap and keep in the fridge overnight.

4. In the morning, the oats will have soaked up the milk and become lovely and creamy. This is the perfect breakfast to take with you on-the-go. Just transfer a portion to a little jar and top it with whatever you like.

🍇 Topping ideas ...
Pomegranate seeds
Fresh berries
Sliced banana

ONION + SUN-DRIED TOMATO MUFFINS

Makes 9

I love cooking savory versions of dishes that are usually sweet. The sun-dried tomatoes, onions, and herbs all work really well together to create a delicious muffin. I either make these for a weekend brunch or in the evening, ready for breakfast the next day.

Ingredients

4 tbsp coconut oil, plus extra for greasing and frying
2½ tbsp milled flaxseed
½ onion, finely diced
1 garlic clove, peeled and crushed
1½ cups (200g) buckwheat flour, sifted
2 tsp baking powder
1 tbsp nutritional yeast (optional)
¼ cup (50g) sun-dried tomatoes in oil, finely chopped
¼ cup (25g) black olives, pitted and finely chopped
1 tsp each of dried rosemary, thyme, and oregano
½ cup (125ml) unsweetened almond milk
¾ cup (150g) unsweetened apple sauce
2 tsp apple cider vinegar
1 tsp baking soda
pink Himalayan salt or sea salt and freshly ground black pepper

1. Preheat the oven to 350°F/180°C. Lightly grease nine holes of a muffin pan with coconut oil and line with baking cups or parchment paper.

2. Mix the flaxseed with 4 tablespoons of water and set it aside to thicken; this will act as the egg.

3. Heat a small amount of coconut oil in a frying pan, add the onion, and fry for 5–7 minutes over medium-high heat, stirring occasionally. Add the garlic and fry for 2 more minutes, then remove from the heat.

4. In a large bowl, mix the flour with the baking powder, nutritional yeast, if using, sun-dried tomatoes, olives, and herbs. Add a pinch of salt and black pepper and mix well.

5. Pour the milk, coconut oil, and apple sauce into a saucepan over medium-low heat and heat gently, until the coconut oil has melted and the milk is warmed, but not boiling. Remove from the heat and keep to one side.

6. In a small bowl, mix the vinegar with the baking soda and stir until it foams; this will help the muffins rise.

7. Add the milk and apple sauce mixture to the bowl of dry ingredients, along with the vinegar and soda mixture, the flaxseed and water, and the cooked onions and garlic.

8. Very gently fold the mixture to combine (this keeps the muffins nice and light—mixing too much can make them tough).

9. Divide the mixture between the baking cups and bake for 25–30 minutes or until a toothpick comes out clean. Remove the pan from the oven and place it on a wire rack to cool.

AVOCADO + STRAWBERRIES ON RYE

Serves 2

Avocado on toast is one of my favorite weekend breakfast choices. It seems to be one of those things that everyone loves. I've livened up my version by adding sweet strawberries and balsamic vinegar.

Ingredients

2 slices of rye bread
8 strawberries, hulled
8–10 mint leaves
1 ripe avocado, pitted
a handful of arugula
balsamic vinegar
freshly ground
   black pepper

1. Toast the rye bread.

2. Slice the strawberries and roughly chop the mint leaves.

3. Slice or mash the avocado and place it on top of the toasted rye bread with the sliced strawberries. Sprinkle over the chopped mint and season with black pepper.

4. Add a handful of arugula, drizzle with balsamic vinegar, and dig in.

CHIA JAMS

I've never understood why some store-bought jams are pumped full of additives. Fruits are abundant in bright colors and flavors, and contain natural sugars, which means you only need a little natural maple syrup to make the jam lovely and sweet. I love this spread on rye bread or crackers, or stirred into oatmeal.

STRAWBERRY

Makes approx. 1 cup

Ingredients

3 cups (350g) strawberries, hulled
2 tbsp chia seeds
2 tbsp lemon juice
2 tbsp maple syrup

1. Roughly chop the strawberries and place them in a medium saucepan with 2 tablespoons water.

2. Set the pan over high heat, bring to a boil, and turn the heat down to medium-low. Mash the strawberries in the pan with a fork and simmer for 5–7 minutes.

3. Remove the pan from the heat and stir in the chia seeds with the lemon juice and maple syrup. Allow the mixture to cool and set for at least 15 minutes before serving. If you prefer a smoother consistency, simply pour the mixture into a blender and blend for a few seconds until smooth.

4. Keep the jam in the fridge in an airtight container for up to 2 weeks.

ORANGE + APRICOT

Makes approx. 1 cup

Ingredients

2 large oranges, peeled
½ cup (80g) fresh apricots
2 tbsp chia seeds
2 tbsp lemon juice
2 tbsp maple syrup

1. Roughly chop the oranges, then halve, pit, and roughly chop the apricots.

2. Place the fruit in a saucepan over low-medium heat. Bring to a boil and simmer for 5 minutes.

3. While the mixture is simmering, use a fork to mash the apricots in the pan.

4. Follow the Strawberry Chia Jam instructions from step 3.

PLUM + GINGER

Makes approx. 1 cup

Ingredients

2 cups (350g) plums, pitted
2-inch piece of fresh ginger,
   peeled and grated
2 tbsp chia seeds
2 tbsp lemon juice
2 tbsp maple syrup

1. Roughly chop the plums and
   place them in a medium saucepan
   with 2 tablespoons of water.

2. Place the pan over medium-low
   heat, bring to a boil, then turn the
   heat down to low, and cover and
   simmer for 10–15 minutes, until
   softened.

3. Once softened, use a fork to
   mash the plums in the pan, and
   add the ginger.

4. Follow the Strawberry Chia Jam
   instructions from step 3.

🥣 Serving ideas ...

Try a teaspoon on top of oatmeal.
Use as a filling for my Jammy Dodgers
(see page 204).
Use as a filling for my Peanut Butter
+ Jam Oat Bars (see page 221).
Spread onto toasted rye bread for
a grab-and-go breakfast.
Spread onto my homemade Oat
Cakes (see page 167).

CHOCOLATE PANCAKES
WITH RASPBERRY SAUCE

Serves 4

I became incredibly excited when I first discovered I could make delicious pancakes that didn't require eggs or dairy. This is the perfect indulgent breakfast for a special occasion. No matter when you serve them, they will impress your friends and family—see if they even notice that they're healthy, too.

Ingredients

pancake batter
1½ cups (200g) buckwheat flour
1½ cups (375ml) unsweetened almond milk
1 ripe banana, peeled
1 tbsp maple syrup
2 tbsp raw cacao powder
1 heaping tbsp chia seeds
½ tsp baking soda
2 tbsp raw cacao nibs
coconut oil

raspberry sauce
1 cup (150g) raspberries
1 tbsp lemon juice
1 tbsp maple syrup
1 tsp all-purpose flour (optional), to thicken

1. Add all the batter ingredients, except for the cacao nibs and coconut oil, to a blender and process to form a smooth batter. Stir in the cacao nibs and let the mixture thicken.

2. Put the raspberries, ¼ cup (60ml) water, lemon juice, and maple syrup into a small saucepan and cook over medium heat, stirring occasionally. When the sauce starts to bubble, turn the heat down to medium and cook for 2–3 minutes until thickened. If it's looking a little too watery, stir in a teaspoon of flour to help the sauce thicken.

3. Heat a little coconut oil in a nonstick frying pan over medium heat. Once hot, pour about ½ cup (125ml) of the pancake batter into the middle of the pan. Cook the pancake for 1–2 minutes on each side and repeat until all the mixture has been used up. You should get 8 pancakes.

4. Stack the pancakes onto plates, drizzle them with the delicious raspberry sauce, and tuck in!

🥣 Serving ideas ...
Swap the raspberries in this sauce with blueberries or strawberries and mix and match the pancakes with the sauces.

COCONUT PANCAKES
WITH MANGO SAUCE

Serves 4

This is one of my most indulgent breakfast recipes, yet it only calls for ingredients that actually provide a whole bunch of health benefits. I love tropical flavors, so it made sense to combine them with one of my favorite breakfasts. It really is like sunshine on a plate.

Ingredients

mango sauce
1 ripe mango, peeled and pitted
a squeeze of lemon juice

pancake batter
1½ cups (150g) rolled oats
2 ripe bananas, peeled
1¼ cups (185ml) unsweetened almond milk
1 tsp apple cider vinegar
1 tbsp coconut nectar or maple syrup
½ tsp organic vanilla extract
1 tsp baking soda
¼ cup (25g) dried unsweetened coconut
coconut oil

topping
1 tbsp dried unsweetened coconut or coconut flakes
a handful of raspberries

1. Start by making the mango sauce. Cut the mango into chunks, add it to a blender with ¼ cup (60ml) water and the lemon juice, and blend until smooth. Transfer the mixture to a bowl and keep it to the side until you're ready to serve.

2. Turn the oats into flour by grinding them in a blender until fine. Transfer the flour to a bowl.

3. Place the bananas, almond milk, apple cider vinegar, coconut nectar, and vanilla extract in the blender and process until smooth.

4. Add the oat flour and baking soda to the banana mixture and blend until smooth. Stir in the ¼ cup of the coconut.

5. Heat a little coconut oil in a nonstick frying pan over medium heat. When the pan is hot, pour a pancake-sized amount of the mixture—around ¼ cup (60ml)—into the center of the pan and cook for about 1–2 minutes on each side, until golden and cooked through. Repeat with the remaining mixture until you have 8 pancakes (if you have a large frying pan you can cook 2–3 at a time).

6. Serve the pancakes topped with the mango sauce, coconut, and raspberries.

➤ Tip ... This makes more sauce than needed. It will keep for 2 days in the fridge.

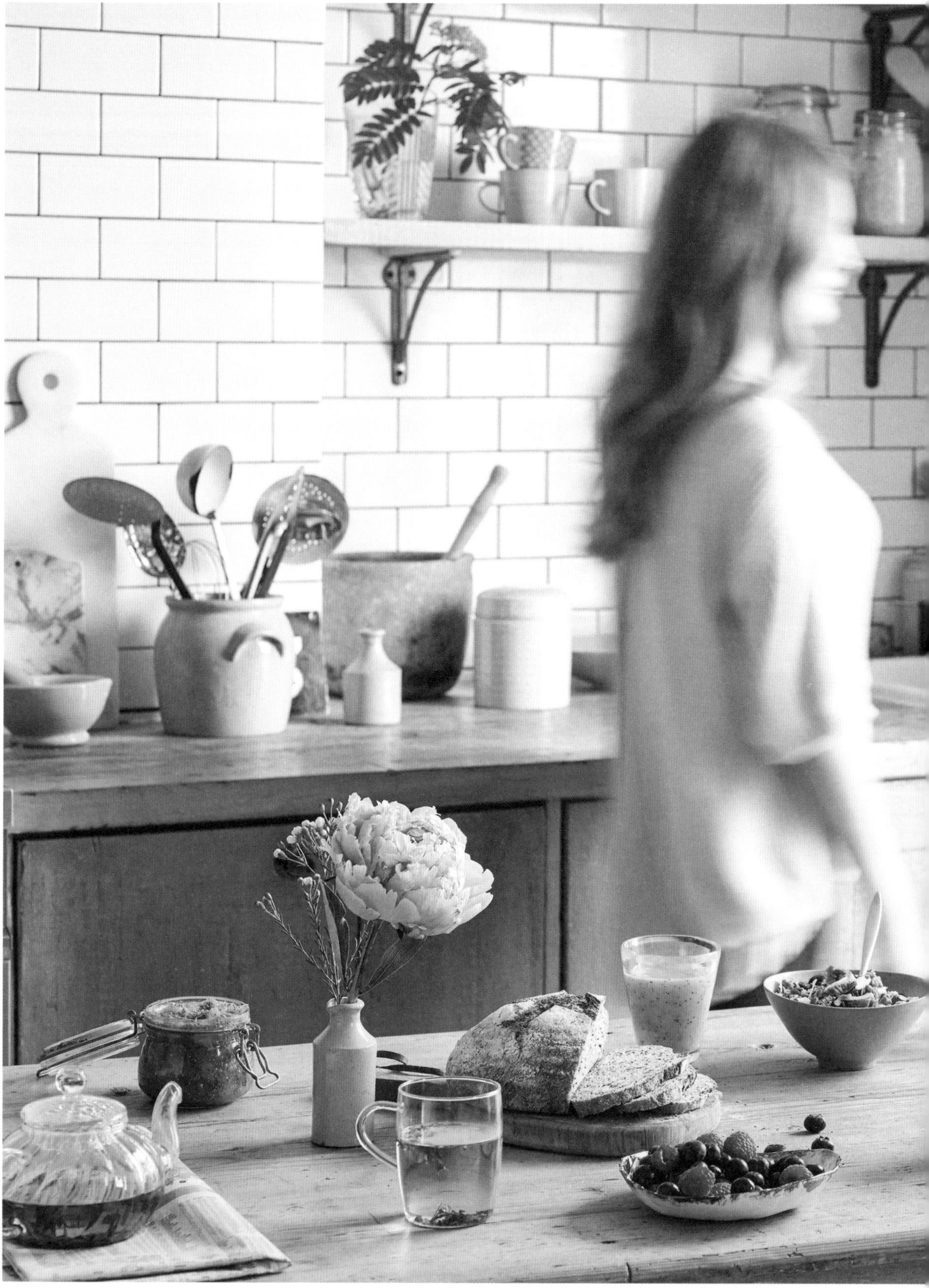

FULL ENGLISH BREAKFAST

Serves 2

People often ask me if I miss out on a full English breakfast, but my version, with garlic mushrooms, grilled vine-ripened cherry tomatoes, baked beans, and tofu scramble, really hits the spot for a filling, hearty breakfast on a Sunday morning, especially after a late night.

Ingredients

grilled tomatoes
6 (250g) ripe cherry
    tomatoes kept on
    the vine
a splash of balsamic
    vinegar

baked beans
1 x 14-oz (400-g) can
    cannellini beans,
    drained
½ tsp onion powder
½ tsp garlic powder
1 x 14-oz (400-g) can
    crushed tomatoes
1 tsp maple syrup
1 tsp blackstrap
    molasses
1 garlic clove, peeled
    and crushed
pink Himalayan salt
    or sea salt and
    freshly ground
    black pepper

garlic mushrooms
1 tbsp coconut oil
10 button mushrooms,
    halved
2 garlic cloves, peeled
    and crushed

1. Put the tofu on a cutting board, place another cutting board on top, and place a heavy pan or plate on top, to press the tofu down and remove excess water. Leave it while you make the beans and mushrooms.

2. To make the beans, simply add all the ingredients to a small saucepan with a pinch of salt and black pepper. Set the pan over medium-high heat and bring it to a boil. Reduce the heat to medium and simmer for 10 minutes, stirring occasionally.

3. Meanwhile, to make the mushrooms, heat the coconut oil in a small frying pan over medium heat and fry the mushrooms for 5 minutes, until they're lightly browned and cooked through, stirring occasionally, and adding the garlic about a minute before the end.

4. Place the cherry tomatoes (still on their vine) on a baking sheet. Sprinkle them with sea salt and a little balsamic vinegar, and put them under the broiler for 3 or 4 minutes, until they start to brown.

5. Once the tofu has been weighed down for 20 minutes, drain any excess liquid, pat the tofu dry with paper towels, and cut it into cubes.

tofu scramble
7 oz (200g)
    firm tofu
1 tsp coconut oil
½ tsp turmeric
½ tsp ground cumin
2 tbsp lemon juice
1 tsp nutritional yeast

toasted rye bread,
    to serve
mashed avocado
    (optional),
    to serve

6. To make the scramble, heat the coconut oil in a frying pan over medium heat. Use your hands to crumble in the tofu, then add the remaining ingredients and cook for about 5 minutes, stirring occasionally.

7. Season to taste and serve everything together with the toasted rye bread and mashed avocado, if you like.

━● Tip ... To save time prepping, you can make the beans in advance and reheat them when you are ready to serve.

CREAMY MUSHROOMS + BEANS ON TOAST

Serves 2

This is a great breakfast to cook on the weekend when you have a bit more time. Baked beans are such a British comfort food, and incredibly easy to make. I've adapted the traditional method by adding a variety of unconventional flavors, such as garlic, and coconut milk for creaminess.

Ingredients

1 tsp coconut oil
2 garlic cloves, peeled and thinly sliced
2 large vine-ripened tomatoes, chopped
6 crimini or portobello mushrooms, thinly sliced
½ x 14-oz (400-g) can coconut milk
½ lemon
2 tbsp finely chopped chives, plus extra to serve
½ x 14-oz (400-g) can cannellini beans, drained
1 tsp paprika
2 slices of rye bread
pink Himalayan salt or sea salt and freshly ground black pepper

1. Heat the oil in a saucepan and fry the garlic and tomatoes for about 3 minutes, stirring occasionally, then add the sliced mushrooms and continue to fry for another 2 minutes, stirring regularly.

2. Pour in the coconut milk, squeeze in the lemon juice, and add the chopped chives and beans. Simmer the mixture over medium-high heat for about 8–12 minutes, until the sauce has thickened. Season to taste with the paprika, salt, and black pepper.

3. Toast the rye bread and pour the creamy mushrooms and beans over the top. Sprinkle with the fresh chives.

➤ Tip ... Keep any leftover lemon juice to make my Morning Detox Water (see page 231).

CARROT + GINGER GRANOLA BARS

Makes 10

I've always loved the combination of carrot and ginger, whether in a juice, a dessert, or a curry! I'm such a grazer, so I love to make things that I can throw in my handbag and grab whenever I'm hungry. These make a lovely, light breakfast to enjoy on the move.

Ingredients

coconut oil,
    for greasing
8 Medjool dates,
    pitted
1½ cups (150g)
    rye flakes
½ cup (60g)
    pumpkin seeds
1 cup (100g) rolled oats
¾ cup (90g) unsalted
    raw walnuts,
    chopped
2 carrots, peeled
    and finely grated
1¼-inch piece of fresh
    ginger, peeled and
    finely grated
3 tsp ground cinnamon
1 tsp turmeric
½ tsp ground nutmeg
½ cup (60g) raisins

1. Preheat the oven to 325°F/170°C. Grease an 8-inch square baking pan with coconut oil and line it with parchment paper.

2. Place the dates with 1 cup (250ml) water in a small saucepan over medium heat and cook for 10 minutes, stirring occasionally.

3. Turn the heat down to low. Use a fork to mash the dates in the pan until they're smooth, then cook for a further 10 minutes, stirring occasionally.

4. Mix together the rye flakes, pumpkin seeds, oats, and walnuts in a large bowl.

5. Stir the carrots and ginger into the date paste with the spices and raisins. Add the mixture to the bowl of dry ingredients and mix well.

6. Pour the mixture into the lined baking pan, smoothing down the top with the back of a spoon, and bake for 35 minutes until golden.

7. Cool in the pan for 10 minutes before cutting into 10 rectangles (this will be easier if it's still warm, but not hot). Store in an airtight container.

━● Tip ... If you don't have any rye flakes, the recipe works just as well if you replace the flakes with 2 cups of oats.

Lunch

02

GREEK ISLAND SALAD

Serves 4

My love for Greek salads began on the beautiful island of Santorini, where my friends and I sat around the pool with a large bowl on our laps every day! I've added a few more ingredients to make it a substantial lunch, and it still transports me back to that Mediterranean sunshine every time I make it.

Ingredients

1 romaine lettuce, sliced into long strips

1 cucumber, diced

4 large vine-ripened tomatoes, diced

1 ripe avocado, peeled, pitted, and diced

½ red onion, sliced

10 black olives, pitted and sliced

5 Medjool dates, pitted and diced

¼ bunch of fresh mint, leaves picked and chopped

1 x 14 oz (400-g) can of chickpeas, drained

a handful of unsalted raw cashews, chopped

2 tbsp each of pumpkin seeds and hemp seeds (optional)

dressing

a squeeze of lime juice

2 tbsp extra-virgin olive oil

1 tbsp balsamic vinegar

1. Place everything into a large bowl, except for the cashews and seeds, if using.

2. In a small bowl, mix together a squeeze of lime juice, the olive oil, and balsamic vinegar. Pour over the salad and toss to coat.

3. Serve sprinkled with the crushed cashews and seeds, if using.

SPICY ASIAN TOFU SALAD

Serves 2

When I was in Mauritius, there was a place that served an incredible cold tofu salad that I became obsessed with! Those flavors inspired this dish. It's not too often that I include soy products in my food, but the tofu here really pulls the whole dish together.

Ingredients

½ 14 oz (400-g) block
  firm tofu
4 oz (100g) buckwheat
  noodles
1 tsp coconut oil
1 carrot, peeled
¼ red cabbage,
  thinly sliced
2 scallions, trimmed
  and sliced
a handful of
  bean sprouts
a large bunch of
  fresh cilantro,
  chopped, with
  a few leaves
  reserved to serve
2 tbsp unsalted raw
  peanuts, chopped,
  to serve
1 tsp sesame seeds,
  to serve

dressing
juice of 1 lime
2 tbsp tamari
1 tsp apple cider
  vinegar
1 tbsp sesame oil
1 tbsp smooth
  peanut butter
½ fresh red chili,
  seeded and sliced

1. Put the tofu on a cutting board, place another cutting board on top, and place a heavy pan or plate on top of that to press the tofu down and remove any excess water. Leave it for about 20 minutes while you cook the noodles.

2. Cook the buckwheat noodles in a pan of boiling water over medium heat for 12 minutes, or according to the package instructions. Drain, rinse under cold water to separate the noodles, and set aside.

3. Once the tofu has been weighed down for 20 minutes, drain any liquid, pat the tofu dry with paper towels, and cut it into cubes.

4. Heat the coconut oil in a frying pan and fry the tofu for 7–10 minutes, stirring occasionally, until golden on all sides.

5. Use a vegetable peeler to peel the carrot into long ribbon-like strips, then mix all the vegetables and cilantro together in a large bowl with the cooled noodles.

6. Make the dressing by combining the lime juice, tamari, vinegar, sesame oil, peanut butter, and chili in a small bowl. Use a fork to whisk it all together.

7. Add the dressing to the salad and stir to coat. Serve topped with the tofu and sprinkled with the chopped peanuts, sesame seeds, and cilantro.

ROASTED FENNEL, LENTIL + FIG SALAD

Serves 2

These flavor combinations are some of my favorites. The distinctive anise taste of fennel and aromatic dill combined with fresh lemon, sweet figs, and the delicate crunch of their seeds creates a wonderful, well-rounded salad. The lentils add real substance to keep you feeling fuller for longer.

Ingredients

½ cup (100g) dried
    Puy lentils, rinsed
1 large fennel bulb
olive oil
3 fresh figs, quartered
a small handful of
    fresh dill, chopped
pink Himalayan salt
    or sea salt and
    freshly ground
    black pepper

dressing
½ lemon
1 tbsp extra-virgin
    olive oil
½ tsp ground cumin

1. Preheat the oven to 350°F/180°C.

2. Place the lentils in a small saucepan, cover the lentils with cold water, and place the pan over medium-high heat. Bring to a boil, then turn the heat down to low, and simmer for 20 minutes, or until the lentils are cooked through, adding more water if needed. Drain, return to the pan, and let cool.

3. Remove any damaged outer leaves from the fennel, cut it into ½-inch wedges and place them in a roasting pan with a drizzle of olive oil and a pinch of salt and black pepper.

4. Roast the fennel for 30–35 minutes, turning the wedges halfway through the cooking time to make sure all of them are evenly cooked. Remove the pan from the oven and allow it to cool.

5. To make the dressing, zest the lemon and set the zest aside. Mix together the extra-virgin olive oil, lemon juice, and cumin in a small bowl.

6. Mix the lentils and fennel together with the dressing and serve with the fig quarters. Sprinkle the chopped dill and a little lemon zest over the top.

MASSAGED KALE CAESAR SALAD

Serves 2

I used to love Caesar salads, but they usually contain little nutritional value, and there are, of course, heaps of dairy in the dressing. I've "superfooded" my salad, so it has an abundance of antioxidants from ingredients such as kale and tahini. What's more, it has a real punch of flavor.

Ingredients

1 lemon
4 tightly packed
    cups (180g) curly
    kale leaves
1 tbsp extra-virgin
    olive oil
½ thick slice of
    rye bread
5 unsalted raw
    cashews, chopped
5 black olives,
    pitted and sliced
6 vine-ripened cherry
    tomatoes, quartered
    (optional)
pink Himalayan salt
    or sea salt

dressing
1 tbsp capers
1 tsp Dijon mustard
2 garlic cloves, peeled
2 tbsp tahini
3 tbsp unsweetened
    almond milk
1 tbsp nutritional yeast
pink Himalayan salt
    or sea salt and
    freshly ground
    black pepper

1. Zest the lemon and keep it to one side. Place the kale in a bowl with the juice of half the lemon, the olive oil, and a pinch of salt. Rub the kale leaves between your fingers for about 3 minutes until they become softer and darker.

2. Add all the dressing ingredients to a small food processor or blender with the juice from the remaining lemon half, and a pinch of salt and pepper. Blend until smooth. Stir 3 tablespoons of the dressing into the kale and mix until well-coated.

3. To make the croutons, toast the rye bread until it's nice and crispy (you may need to toast the bread twice). Cut the toasted rye bread into small cubes.

4. Combine the dressed kale with the chopped cashews, sliced olives, lemon zest, and the cherry tomatoes, if using. Scatter the croutons over the salad before serving.

GRAIN SALADS—3 WAYS

Grains make the perfect salad for summer—ideal for picnics! These are easy recipes using super healthy quinoa, pearl barley, and bulgur wheat, with lots of fresh herbs, vegetables, and spices for flavor. They make a lovely alternative to rice salads, and are also great as side dishes.

ROASTED ASPARAGUS + BEET SALAD WITH PEARL BARLEY

Serves 2

Ingredients

2 beets (about 160g)
¼ cup (50g) pearl barley, rinsed
4 asparagus spears
olive oil
2 large handfuls of watercress
4 unsalted raw Brazil nuts, chopped
pink Himalayan salt or sea salt
    and freshly ground black pepper

dressing
2 tbsp balsamic vinegar
2 tbsp extra-virgin olive oil
juice of ½ orange
pink Himalayan salt or sea salt and
    freshly ground black pepper

1. Preheat the oven to 400°F/200°C.

2. Trim the ends off the beets, wrap each one in tin foil, and bake for 40 minutes.

3. Place the barley in a saucepan with 1½ cups (375ml) cold water. Cover, bring to a boil, and simmer over medium heat for 40 minutes, until soft, or according to package instructions. Set aside to cool.

4. Slice the woody ends off the asparagus and slice lengthwise into long, thin ribbons. Rub with a small amount of olive oil, salt, and black pepper, and place on a baking pan. Cook in the oven with the beets for the last 10 minutes of cooking time, turning halfway through.

5. Allow the beets to cool, then peel off the skin, and slice them into eighths.

6. To make the dressing, place the ingredients in a cup and whisk with a fork.

7. Use a fork to fluff up the pearl barley and serve it over the watercress. Add the roasted beets and asparagus and finish with a drizzle of the dressing and a handful of chopped Brazil nuts.

➤● Tip ... Use golden or pink beets here if you can get them. They taste beautiful.

BULGUR WHEAT TABBOULEH

Serves 2

Ingredients

¼ cup (40g) bulgur wheat
a small handful of kale, chopped
a couple of sprigs of fresh mint,
    leaves picked and finely chopped
½ bunch of fresh parsley, leaves
    picked and finely chopped
2 large vine-ripened tomatoes, diced
1 scallion, finely sliced
½ cucumber, sliced lengthwise
    into eighths and chopped
½ lemon
1 tbsp extra-virgin olive oil
2 tbsp pomegranate seeds
pink Himalayan salt or sea salt and
    freshly ground black pepper

1. Cook the bulgur wheat according to
    the package instructions, then drain,
    and let cool in a serving bowl.

2. Once cool, mix in all the chopped
    vegetables and herbs. Zest the lemon
    half and set the zest aside. Squeeze
    the juice into the bowl, add the olive
    oil, and season with salt and black
    pepper.

3. Sprinkle over the lemon zest and
    pomegranate seeds and serve.

━━● Tip … To remove pomegranate
seeds, try the water method—cut the
pomegranate in half, place the halves in
a bowl of water, and break them apart
with your hands.

AVOCADO + TURMERIC SALAD WITH QUINOA

Serves 2

Ingredients

¾ cup (150g) quinoa, rinsed
1 avocado, peeled and pitted
¼ cup (40g) sun-dried
    tomatoes, in oil
1 tsp turmeric
¼ tsp ground cumin
a pinch of cayenne pepper
¼ bunch fresh cilantro,
    chopped
a squeeze of lime juice
pink Himalayan salt or sea salt and
    freshly ground black pepper

1. Place the quinoa in a saucepan
    with 1½ cups (375ml) water. Cook
    over medium heat, bring to a boil,
    then turn the heat down to low,
    and simmer for 15 minutes until the
    water has been absorbed and the
    quinoa is cooked, adding more water
    if needed. Set aside to cool.

2. Chop the avocado into chunks. Rinse
    the oil off the sun-dried tomatoes
    and slice them into strips.

3. When the quinoa has cooled, fluff it
    up with a fork and stir in the spices.
    Stir in most of the cilantro, avocado,
    and sun-dried tomatoes, and add a
    squeeze of lime juice.

4. Add salt and pepper to taste, then
    serve scattered with the remaining
    cilantro leaves.

WARMING SQUASH SOUP

Serves 4

This soup is the ultimate winter warmer. When it's frosty outside, I love to snuggle up on my sofa with a chunky-knitted blanket and a bowl of this soup. It is deliciously creamy from the coconut milk and full of flavor with a hint of spiciness from the herbs and fresh vegetables.

Ingredients

1 tsp coconut oil
1 onion, diced
1 garlic clove, peeled
  and crushed
½ fresh red chili,
  seeded and
  chopped
1 tsp ground cumin
1 tsp dried thyme
½ tsp ground
  coriander
1 small butternut
  squash, peeled
  and chopped
2 carrots, peeled
  and chopped
½ 14-oz (400-g) can
  coconut milk
pink Himalayan salt
  or sea salt and
  freshly ground
  black pepper
a handful of cilantro,
  to serve

1. Heat the coconut oil in a large saucepan over medium-low heat and gently fry the diced onion for about 5 minutes.

2. Add the garlic, chili, cumin, thyme, and cilantro and fry for another minute. Pour in 5 cups (1.25 liters) boiling water; add the squash, carrots, and most of the coconut milk; and simmer for about 20 minutes or until the vegetables have softened.

3. Season with salt and black pepper and blend until smooth. Serve sprinkled with fresh cilantro leaves and a drizzle of the remaining coconut milk.

➤ Tip ... My soups serve 4 people, so when I'm cooking just for me, I make a batch and freeze the remaining portions for later.

KALE MINESTRONE

Serves 4

It can be hard to find simple plant-based food in Italy, but I love the flavors of that country. I decided to create a comforting minestrone soup using spelt pasta and kale. For me, every meal should be packed with ingredients that are good for our bodies, which is why I included a dark leafy green here.

Ingredients

1 onion, diced
1 tbsp olive oil
2 garlic cloves, crushed
2 carrots, peeled and diced
2 celery stalks, chopped
1 yellow bell pepper, seeded and diced
1 tsp dried oregano
1 organic low-sodium vegetable bouillon cube
1 x 14-oz (400-g) can cannellini beans, drained
2 x 14-oz (400-g) cans chopped tomatoes
1 tbsp tomato purée
6 oz (175g) spelt spaghetti
2 cups tightly packed kale leaves
pink Himalayan salt or sea salt and freshly ground black pepper
a small handful of fresh basil leaves, chopped, to serve

1. In a large saucepan, fry the onion in the olive oil over medium heat for 5–7 minutes until softened.

2. Add the garlic, carrots, celery, and pepper and fry for an additional 5 minutes. Add the oregano and a pinch of salt and black pepper.

3. Dissolve the bouillon cube in 2 cups (500ml) boiling water and pour it into the saucepan with the beans, canned tomatoes, and tomato purée. Bring to a boil and simmer for 40 minutes.

4. Break the spaghetti into 1-inch pieces, add them to the pan, and continue to simmer for an additional 10 minutes, adding 1–2 cups (250–500ml) more water if needed.

5. Stir in the kale and simmer for 5 more minutes.

6. Serve sprinkled with the fresh basil.

Tip ... To make this gluten-free, simply replace the spelt spaghetti with your favorite gluten-free pasta—I love brown rice penne.

SWEET CORN CHOWDER IN SPELT SOURDOUGH

Serves 4

On a visit to San Francisco in 2013, I tried the famous clam chowder that's served in a sourdough bread bowl. This is my healthy version. It's totally carbolicious, but it's a showstopper presented in the sourdough. Once you're halfway through the soup, break off the bread and dip it in.

Ingredients

1 organic low-sodium vegetable bouillon cube
⅔ cup (150ml) oat milk or other non-dairy milk
¼ cup (60ml) white wine
2 medium potatoes, peeled and diced
1 tsp coconut oil
1 onion, diced
1 leek, trimmed and chopped
3 garlic cloves, peeled and finely chopped
2 sprigs of fresh thyme, leaves picked
1 tbsp whole-wheat flour
1 celery stalk, trimmed and diced
2 ears of corn, husked
a squeeze of lemon juice
pink Himalayan salt or sea salt and freshly ground black pepper
4 small round spelt or whole-wheat sourdough loaves
a couple of sprigs of fresh parsley, leaves picked and chopped, to serve

1. Pour 2 cups (500ml) water into a large saucepan and crumble in the bouillon cube. Add the oat milk, wine, and potatoes. Set over medium-high heat, bring to a boil, then simmer for 15–20 minutes until the potatoes are just cooked.

2. Meanwhile, heat the coconut oil in a frying pan over medium-high heat and fry the onion, leek, and garlic with the thyme leaves for a few minutes until softened.

3. Coat the vegetables with flour, then add the pan-fried vegetables to the saucepan along with the celery.

4. Cut the corn kernels off the cobs and add the corn to the pan. Season with a decent amount of salt and black pepper and add a squeeze of lemon juice. Simmer for 5 more minutes, then remove from the heat.

5. To make the bread bowls cut a circle out of the top of the bread loaves and scoop out the bread to make them hollow.

6. Pour the chowder into the bread bowls and sprinkle with the fresh parsley.

➙ Tip ... If you can't find the right size sourdough roll, simply serve the soup in a bowl with a slice of nice sourdough on the side.

FARMHOUSE VEGETABLE SOUP

Serves 4

Ideally, this soup would be made in a rustic farmhouse kitchen using vegetables from the garden, but unfortunately this is hugely unrealistic for me, because I live in London. Nonetheless, you can still get the same flavors with a few simple, fresh ingredients.

Ingredients

1 tbsp coconut oil
3 carrots, peeled
   and chopped
2 celery stalks,
   chopped
2 leeks, trimmed
   and chopped
1 potato (about 7 oz
   or 200g), peeled
   and chopped
1 parsnip, peeled
   and chopped
1 small head of
   broccoli, chopped
1 organic low-sodium
   vegetable bouillon
   cube
½ cup (100g) pearl
   barley, rinsed
2 bay leaves
3 sprigs of fresh thyme
pink Himalayan salt
   or sea salt and
   freshly ground
   black pepper

1. Heat the oil in a large saucepan over medium-high heat and fry all the vegetables for about 10 minutes, until softened, stirring often and adding a splash of water if the vegetables are scorching.

2. Dissolve the bouillon cube in 4 cups (1 liter) boiling water and pour it into the pan with the pearl barley, bay leaves, thyme sprigs, and a pinch of salt and pepper.

3. Cover and simmer for 30–40 minutes, or until the barley is soft. Remove the bay leaves and thyme sprigs and serve.

CREAMY CARROT SOUP
WITH ROASTED BROCCOLI

Serves 4

One of my favorite lunch choices, soup is quick and easy to make and a great way to get an abundance of nutritious vegetables into your diet. This carrot soup is creamy and velvety smooth, and when paired with fiery garlic-roasted broccoli, it all comes to life.

Ingredients

2 tbsp coconut oil
½ head of broccoli, chopped into florets
4 tbsp lemon juice
1 tsp dried chili flakes
4 garlic cloves, peeled and finely chopped
2 onions, diced
4 large carrots, peeled and sliced into discs
¼ bunch of fresh thyme, leaves picked
1 tsp paprika
4 cups (1 liter) unsweetened almond milk
pink Himalayan salt or sea salt and freshly ground black pepper

1. Preheat the oven to 400°F/200°C.

2. Put half the coconut oil in a large roasting pan and place the pan in the oven for a few seconds to melt the coconut oil. Add the broccoli, toss with the lemon juice and chili flakes, and roast for 15 minutes. Add two-thirds of the garlic halfway through the cooking time.

3. Heat the remaining coconut oil in a large saucepan over medium-low heat. Add the onions and fry for 3–5 minutes. Add the remaining garlic and fry for an additional minute.

4. Add the carrots and cook for 6 minutes, then stir in the thyme leaves with the paprika. Pour in 2 cups (500ml) water with the almond milk. Turn the heat up to medium-high, bring to a boil, then simmer uncovered for about 15 minutes until the carrots have softened.

5. Taste and season the mixture with salt and black pepper, then blend until it is totally smooth.

6. Reheat the soup in the saucepan, if necessary, then serve it with the roasted broccoli and garlic sprinkled on top.

GAZPACHO

Serves 2

I spent a lot of my childhood in the Costa Del Sol, in Spain, with my family. An ongoing joke, whenever we're there, is that we all order the same thing at lunch: a bowl of gazpacho. My version of this smooth, chilled vegetable soup is so refreshing in the summer heat and is packed with flavor.

Ingredients

1 cucumber,
  roughly chopped
10 vine-ripened
  tomatoes, quartered
1 red bell pepper,
  seeded and
  roughly chopped
½ green bell pepper,
  seeded and roughly
  chopped
3 garlic cloves, peeled
  and roughly
  chopped
½ onion, roughly
  chopped
1 tbsp apple
  cider vinegar
  or lemon juice
¼ cup (60ml) extra-
  virgin olive oil
¼–½ tsp cayenne
  pepper

1. Add all the vegetables to a blender, reserving a small chunk each of cucumber, pepper, and onion.

2. Add the vinegar, olive oil, cayenne pepper, and 1 cup (250ml) water, and blend until smooth.

3. Strain the gazpacho into a large bowl or pitcher, using a wooden spoon to press the soup through the sieve if it slows down.

4. Chill the gazpacho for at least 3 hours.

5. Finely dice the reserved cucumber, pepper, and onion.

6. Once cooled, serve the gazpacho in bowls sprinkled with the diced vegetables.

➤ Tip ... If you have a juicer, use it to blend the gazpacho ingredients and skip step 3.

RAW PEA + ZUCCHINI SOUP

Serves 2

I made this raw soup for my first ever food demonstration. You may be wary of a raw green soup, but trust me on this one! It's so simple to make, and doesn't require any more effort than making a smoothie. Serve this soup cold to keep the nutrient value as high as possible.

Ingredients

½ cup (75g)
    frozen peas
½ zucchini
1 ripe avocado,
    peeled and pitted
1 scallion, trimmed
1 garlic clove, peeled
2 tbsp lemon juice
5 fresh mint leaves,
    plus extra to serve
¼ tsp cayenne
    pepper, plus a
    pinch to serve
pink Himalayan salt
    or sea salt and
    freshly ground
    black pepper
1 tbsp sliced
    almonds, to serve

1. Place all the ingredients, except for the almonds, into a blender, along with 1 cup (250ml) water. Blend until totally smooth and creamy, adding more water if you prefer a thinner consistency.

2. Season with salt and pepper to taste and serve with the sliced almonds, extra mint leaves, and cayenne pepper sprinkled on top.

Tip ... Spring Garden Risotto (see page 144), is a great recipe for using up the leftover zucchini.

CHINESE CAULIFLOWER
RICE WITH BOK CHOY

Serves 4

One of my old guilty pleasures was fried rice ordered from the local Chinese take-out restaurant. I loved it. That's what inspired me to make this Asian lunchtime dish full of goodness; I find rice to be quite heavy sometimes, so when I want something light, cauliflower is a great alternative.

Ingredients

cauliflower rice

1 head of cauliflower, quartered
1 tbsp sliced almonds
1 tbsp dried unsweetened coconut
1 tbsp sesame oil
1 garlic clove, peeled and crushed
1 fresh red chili, seeded and chopped
2 tbsp tamari
½ tsp ground cinnamon
1-inch piece of fresh ginger, peeled and chopped
½ onion, peeled and chopped
1 x 6-oz (190g) can sweet corn, drained
1½ cups (200g) frozen peas
a handful of bean sprouts
¼ bunch of fresh cilantro, leaves picked, to serve

1. Grate the cauliflower with a box grater, or pulse in a food processor until it forms a consistency similar to rice.

2. In a small dry frying pan over medium-high heat, toast the sliced almonds for a minute or two, until lightly browned, and add the coconut halfway through the cooking time. Toss often (it's easy to burn the coconut, so keep an eye on it!). Transfer to a plate and set aside.

3. Place a wok or large frying pan over medium heat, add the sesame oil and cook, stirring regularly, the garlic, chili, tamari, cinnamon, ginger, and onion for a couple of minutes.

4. Now add the cauliflower rice, sweet corn, and peas. Stir until all the ingredients are mixed together and cook, stirring often, for about 10–15 minutes, adding the bean sprouts in the last 5 minutes.

5. While the rice is cooking, heat the coconut oil in a large frying pan or wok over medium heat. Add the broccolini and cook for 5–7 minutes, stirring, until it is cooked, but still has a bit of bite, then transfer it to a plate.

bok choy

1 tbsp coconut oil
7 oz (200g) broccolini
1-inch piece of
   fresh ginger, peeled
   and finely chopped
½ fresh red chili,
   seeded and
   finely chopped
3 small bok choy,
   quartered
   lengthwise

6. Add the ginger and chili to the wok or pan with
   the bok choy (you may have to do this in batches).
   Fry for a few minutes until cooked, then add the
   broccolini back into the pan and toss.

7. Serve in bowls with the cauliflower rice,
   sprinkled with the cilantro leaves, toasted
   almonds, and coconut.

Tip ... A handful of green vegetables, like snow
peas or sugar snap peas, would be lovely in this recipe,
too. Simply add them to the pan with the bok choy.

JAPANESE MISO EGGPLANTS

Serves 2

One of my favorite Japanese restaurants in London introduced me to miso eggplants. They're packed with flavor and are far more filling than they seem at first glance. If you want something to go with these, I would recommend some brown rice and stir-fried broccolini with garlic.

Ingredients

2 eggplants
olive oil
1 heaping tbsp brown
   rice miso
1 tsp coconut sugar
1 tbsp tamari
1 half-inch piece of
   fresh ginger, peeled
   and finely chopped
2 tsp sesame seeds,
   to serve
1 scallion, finely
chopped, to serve

1. Preheat the oven to 350°F/180°C.

2. Halve the eggplants lengthwise, keeping the stalks intact. Score the cut side with criss-crosses about one-quarter inch wide. Brush lightly with olive oil and bake for 35 minutes.

3. Add the miso to a saucepan over high heat with ¼ cup (60ml) water, the coconut sugar, tamari, and chopped ginger. Stir to combine.

4. Bring to a boil and continue to boil for 5–7 minutes until reduced and thickened.

5. When the eggplants have been baking for 35 minutes, remove them from the oven and spread 1 tablespoon of the miso mixture over each half. Bake the eggplant for an additional 5 minutes until it's bubbling.

6. Remove the eggplant from the oven and serve with a scattering of sesame seeds and scallions.

🥄 Serving ideas ...

Try these eggplants with cooked wild rice tossed in lime juice and chopped cilantro, or with my Spicy Asian Tofu Salad (see page 70).

ROASTED PEPPER + ONION PESTO TART
Serves 6–8

This is a great dish to make ahead of time. When I'm busy, I often find it hard to make lunch from scratch, so I sometimes make it the night before, so I know I will have something wholesome, filling, and tasty, ready to eat, and won't end up buying something less nutritious on the go.

Ingredients

topping
olive oil
2 red onions, peeled, and cut into 8 wedges
3 red or yellow peppers, seeded and sliced

sweet potato crust
1 small sweet potato 7 oz or (200g), peeled
1 cup (150g) spelt flour, plus extra for dusting
1 cup (150g) whole-wheat flour
¼ cup (60ml) olive oil
pink Himalayan salt or sea salt

brazil nut pesto
2 garlic cloves, peeled
1½ cups (225g) unsalted raw Brazil nuts
3 large handfuls of fresh basil leaves
3 large handfuls of spinach
3 tbsp apple cider vinegar
⅜ cup (100ml) extra-virgin olive oil

1. Preheat the oven to 350°F/180°C. Grease and flour an 8 x 8-inch shallow baking pan with olive oil.

2. Place the onion wedges and pepper slices in a roasting pan, drizzle with olive oil, and roast in the oven for 40 minutes, tossing occasionally, until cooked through and browned.

3. To make the crust, chop the sweet potato into chunks and steam for 15 minutes. Allow to cool.

4. Mix together the flours and a pinch of salt, then stir in the olive oil and ¼ cup (60ml) water. Mash the sweet potato and use your hands to fully combine it with the flour mixture to form a dough.

5. Roll out the dough to cover the bottom of the pan. Gently press the dough so it covers the outer edges and corners. Use a knife to scrape away the excess from the edges. Add parchment paper and pie weights on top of the crust and bake it for 15 minutes.

6. Meanwhile, make the pesto by adding all the pesto ingredients, except 2 tbsp of the Brazil nuts, to a food processor and blend for 1–2 minutes or until smooth.

7. Remove the paper and pie weights after 15 minutes, then return the crust to the oven for 5 more minutes.

8. Remove the crust from the oven and generously spread the pesto on top of the crust. Add the roasted vegetables, chop and sprinkle the reserved Brazil nuts on top, and bake for a further 5–7 minutes until golden and cooked through. Serve hot or cold with a lovely green salad.

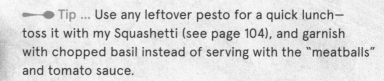

Tip ... Use any leftover pesto for a quick lunch—
toss it with my Squashetti (see page 104), and garnish
with chopped basil instead of serving with the "meatballs"
and tomato sauce.

Dinner

03

MEXICAN CHILI BOWL
Serves 2

Mexican is one of my favorite cuisines. This is a twist on the popular classic chili con carne. I love recreating traditional comfort foods, all made from wholesome ingredients. I've replaced rice with quinoa, sour cream with sour coconut cream, and loaded the chili with vegetables and beans.

Ingredients

1 onion, diced
1 tsp coconut oil
2 garlic cloves, peeled
   and crushed
1 red bell pepper,
   seeded and
   sliced into strips
6 button mushrooms,
   chopped
¼ cup (60ml) red wine
   or vegetable stock
1 tsp yeast extract
1 x 14-oz (400-g) can
   chopped tomatoes
2 tbsp tomato purée
1 x 14-oz (400-g) can
   kidney beans,
   drained
1 bay leaf
1 tsp ground cumin
½ tsp paprika
1 tsp dried oregano
1 tsp dried thyme
½ tsp chili powder
¾ cup (150g)
   quinoa, rinsed
½ organic low-sodium
   vegetable
   bouillon cube
pink Himalayan salt
   or sea salt and
   freshly ground
   black pepper

sour coconut cream

1 x 14-oz (400-g) can
   coconut milk,
   refrigerated
2 tbsp nutritional yeast
a squeeze of
   lemon juice

1. Fry the onion in the coconut oil over a medium heat for 5–7 minutes, until softened. Add the crushed garlic and continue to fry for another couple of minutes.

2. Add the bell pepper, mushrooms, red wine or vegetable stock, and the yeast extract. Turn the heat down to medium-low and simmer for 5 minutes.

3. Add the diced tomatoes, tomato purée, and kidney beans with the bay leaf and remaining spices and herbs. Season with a pinch of salt and black pepper.

4. Bring to a boil, then simmer over medium-low heat for 15–20 minutes, until thickened.

5. Place the quinoa in a saucepan over medium heat. Boil off the excess water for about 30–45 seconds to help remove the quinoa's earthy taste, but don't let it burn. Add 1½ cups (375ml) cold water and the bouillon cube and bring the mixture to a boil. Simmer for 15 minutes until the liquid is absorbed, adding more water if needed. Set aside to cool.

6. To make the sour cream, scoop out half the solid coconut cream that has risen to the top of the can of coconut milk (this should be around ⅓ cup or 75g) and whisk with the other sour cream ingredients in a large bowl.

7. Serve the chili with the quinoa and sour cream and dig in.

🥣 Serving ideas ...
Summer Salsa (see page 158).
Guacamole (see page 158).
Black Bean Dip (see page 163).
A small handful of cilantro leaves.

BEET BURGERS

Serves 4

Veggie burgers are a common alternative at barbecues and picnics, but I often find they're bland and heavy. I've created these using beets for a different texture, with a hint of sweetness from apricots and mild spiciness from the cayenne pepper.

Ingredients

3 beets, peeled and grated
1 tsp coconut oil
1 red onion, chopped
2 garlic cloves, peeled and crushed
2½ tbsp milled flaxseed
1 x 14-oz (400-g) can cannellini beans, drained
4 unsulphured dried apricots
¼ cup (30g) pumpkin seeds
2 tbsp lemon juice
1 tsp dried oregano
¼ tsp cayenne pepper
1 tsp ground cumin
pink Himalayan salt or sea salt and freshly ground black pepper
8 large red leaf or Boston lettuce leaves, to serve
2 ripe beefsteak tomatoes, sliced, to serve
2 ripe avocados, sliced, to serve
2 large radishes, sliced, to serve
whole grain mustard, to serve

1. Preheat the oven to 375ºF/190ºC.

2. Use paper towels to roughly dry the grated beets.

3. Heat the coconut oil in a frying pan and fry the onion for 5 minutes, until softened. Then add the garlic, fry for another minute, remove the pan from the heat, and set it aside.

4. Mix together the flaxseed and 3 tablespoons of water in a small bowl and set it aside to thicken.

5. In a food processor, pulse the beans, apricots, and pumpkin seeds a few times—you want it to be still relatively chunky. Add the lemon juice, dried oregano, cayenne pepper, and cumin with a pinch of salt and black pepper and pulse again.

6. Place the bean mixture in a large bowl, add the grated beet, flaxseed mixture, and onion, and mix together.

7. Take a quarter of the mixture and form a ball. Lay it on a baking sheet and gently press down to form a patty. Repeat three more times.

8. Bake the burgers in the oven for 40 minutes, flipping them over halfway through the cooking time.

9. Once cooked, serve the burgers in the lettuce leaves with sliced tomato, avocado, sliced radish, and a little whole grain mustard.

🥣 Serving ideas ...
Serve with my Spiced Wedges (see page 150) and my Homemade Tomato Ketchup (see page 154).

SQUASHETTI + "MEATBALLS"

Serves 4

Rather than looking at healthy eating as missing out, think of it as altering your favorite meals so that you can load your body with goodness, while still satisfying your taste buds. Here, pasta is made from vibrant, nutritious butternut squash and the "meatballs" from protein-rich whole foods.

Ingredients

"meatballs"
½ cup (100g) dried
    Puy or French green
    lentils
1 onion, finely diced
1 teaspoon coconut oil
1 garlic clove, peeled
    and diced
1 cup (100g) unsalted
    raw walnuts
½ x 14-oz (400-g) can
    black beans,
    drained and rinsed
2 tbsp buckwheat flour
1 tsp dried oregano
1 tsp dried basil
8 unsulphured dried
    apricots, finely
    diced

squashetti
2 butternut squash
    (approx. 1¼ lb or
    1.2kg each)
olive oil

1 x Tomato Sauce recipe,
    (see page 109)
pink Himalayan salt
    or sea salt and
    freshly ground
    black pepper
a handful of fresh basil
    leaves, to serve
a sprinkling of
    nutritional yeast
    (optional)

1. Preheat the oven to 350°F/180°C.

2. Start by making the "meatballs." Rinse and drain the lentils, put them into a saucepan, and cover with water. Place the saucepan over medium-high heat and bring to a boil. Turn the heat down to low and simmer for 30 minutes until cooked or according to the package instructions.

3. Fry half the onion in the coconut oil for 6–8 minutes, until softened, adding the garlic for the final minute.

4. In a food processor, pulse the walnuts a couple of times until they are in small chunks. Add the remaining meatball ingredients, except the reserved onion and apricots, along with a pinch of salt and black pepper, the cooked onion, garlic, and lentils. Blend until combined. Stir in the reserved raw diced onion and apricots.

5. Form the meatball mixture into 12 ping-pong-sized balls and place them on a baking pan. Bake for 30 minutes, turning the meatballs halfway through the cooking time.

6. Peel both butternut squash and use a spiralizer to turn the squash into noodles. Transfer to a baking dish, drizzle with olive oil, toss to coat, and bake for about 10 minutes, turning every couple of minutes.

7. Serve the squashetti in bowls, pour over the tomato sauce, add the meatballs, and serve sprinkled with fresh basil leaves and nutritional yeast, if using.

MAURITIAN MASALA WITH COCONUT CILANTRO RICE

Serves 2

When I traveled to Mauritius, I was blown away by the food. With influences from Africa, France, India, and China, it was like nothing I'd ever tasted or seen before. I've adapted this traditional curry, but the fundamentals of Mauritian cooking are still at the core of this recipe.

Ingredients

1 cup (200g) brown rice, rinsed
1 tsp coconut oil
1 onion, diced
3 fresh or 6–8 dried curry leaves
2 garlic cloves, peeled and crushed
2-inch piece of fresh ginger, peeled and grated
1 tbsp medium curry powder
1 tbsp turmeric
2 tsp ground cumin
1 cup (200g) butternut squash, peeled and diced
1 tbsp fresh thyme leaves, chopped
1 fresh green chili, seeded and diced
1 small zucchini, diced
1 red bell pepper, seeded and thinly sliced
2 tbsp chopped fresh cilantro
2 tbsp dried unsweetened coconut
pink Himalayan salt or sea salt
1 scallion, trimmed and sliced, to serve

1. Place the rice in a saucepan, cover with water, and bring to a boil over high heat. Turn the heat down to medium-low and simmer for 25 minutes or according to the package instructions.

2. Heat the coconut oil in a frying pan over medium heat and fry the onion with the curry leaves for about 5 minutes.

3. Add the crushed garlic and ginger and continue to fry until the onion is golden. Stir in the spices to coat the onion.

4. Add the squash with the thyme leaves, chili, and about ½ cup (125ml) water and stir well. Season with a pinch of salt and cook for a couple of minutes.

5. Now add the zucchini and bell pepper with 1 cup (250ml) of water and simmer for about 20–25 minutes until the squash is tender. Feel free to add more water, depending on the consistency.

6. Once the rice is cooked, stir in most of the chopped cilantro and all of the coconut.

7. Serve the curry with the rice, sprinkled with sliced scallions and the remaining fresh cilantro.

→ Tip ... If you want to feed more people, this recipe is easy to scale up. For a larger yield, simmer the curry a little longer.

BUTTERNUT SQUASH PIZZA CRUST

You'd think that pizza would be the first thing to go when you start eating healthily, but with this recipe you can make one that the entire family will enjoy, even the biggest cheese and meat fans. I've created three different toppings, all with the same crust made from butternut squash.

Ingredients

½ butternut squash (approx. 1½ lb), peeled and chopped
2 tbsp milled flaxseed
2 cups (250g) buckwheat flour
1 tsp mixed herbs
1 tsp dried oregano
1 tbsp coconut oil, plus extra for greasing
pink Himalayan salt or sea salt and freshly ground black pepper

1. Preheat the oven to 350°F/180°C.

2. Steam the squash for 15–20 minutes, until soft, and transfer to a large mixing bowl.

3. In a small bowl, mix the flaxseed with 4 tablespoons of water and set it aside for a few minutes to thicken up and form a gel.

4. Mash the squash until smooth, then stir in the flour with a pinch of salt and black pepper, the dried herbs, the thickened flaxseed, and coconut oil. Mix together until the dough begins to form. It will be wet, but don't worry, it firms up as it bakes.

5. Grease a baking pan or a round pizza pan with a little coconut oil and smoothly spread the dough onto it, using the back of a wooden spoon. Bake the crust for 30 minutes, until lightly brown and crisp around the edges.

BUTTERNUT SQUASH PIZZA—3 WAYS

PESTO, TOMATO + BASIL

Serves 2

Ingredients

1 x Basil Pesto recipe (see page 159)
1 large vine-ripened tomato,
    thinly sliced
1 tbsp pine nuts
pink Himalayan salt or sea salt and
    freshly ground black pepper
a handful of fresh basil leaves,
    to serve

1. When the butternut squash pizza
   crust is cooked, remove it from the
   oven and cover with the pesto.
   Add the tomato slices and pine nuts
   and bake for another 10 minutes.
   Serve with the basil leaves sprinkled
   on top.

RED ONION, CHERRY TOMATO + ARUGULA

Serves 2

Ingredients

1 x Tomato Sauce (see right)
¼ red onion, thinly sliced
¼ fresh red chili, thinly sliced
6 ripe cherry tomatoes, halved
a handful of arugula leaves

1. Spread the Tomato Sauce over the
   baked butternut squash pizza crust.
   Add the sliced onion, chili, and
   cherry tomatoes. Bake for 10 more
   minutes.

2. Serve sprinkled with arugula.

MUSHROOM, RED PEPPER + OLIVE

Serves 2

Ingredients

tomato sauce
½ red onion, diced
1 tsp coconut oil
4 large vine-ripened tomatoes, chopped
1 garlic clove, peeled and chopped
1 tsp dried oregano
½ tsp honey or maple syrup
a handful of fresh basil leaves

toppings
2 mushrooms, thinly sliced
3 black olives, pitted and sliced
½ red bell pepper, sliced
½ tsp dried chili flakes
½ tsp dried oregano

1. While the crust is baking, make the
   tomato sauce. To make the tomato
   sauce, fry the red onion in the
   coconut oil over medium heat
   for 5 minutes until soft.

2. Add the remaining sauce ingredients
   and cook, stirring, over low heat
   for about 15 minutes. Then allow to
   cool. Pour the sauce into a blender
   and blend until smooth.

3. Spread the tomato sauce over the
   baked butternut squash pizza crust
   and add the toppings. Bake the pizza
   for 10 more minutes.

MEXICAN WILD RICE LETTUCE WRAPS

Serves 4

These wraps are a fun way to eat healthily—place all the different components on the table so everyone can help themselves. I love Mexican food, so I wanted to make a healthier version of the popular fajita, without losing any flavor or color.

Ingredients

2 red onions, sliced
2 bell peppers, seeded
    and sliced
2 tbsp olive oil
pink Himalayan salt
    or sea salt and
    freshly ground
    black pepper
2 large portobello
    mushrooms, sliced
4 ears of corn, husked
1 cup (200g) wild
    rice, rinsed
1 x 14-oz (400-g) can
    chopped tomatoes
½ fresh red chili
    pepper, seeded and
    chopped
1 head of lettuce,
    to serve
2 ripe avocados,
    peeled, pitted
    and sliced, to serve
Summer Salsa, to
    serve (see page 158)
Cashew Cheese, to
    serve (see page 159)

spice mix
½ tsp ground cumin
½ tsp dried basil
¼ tsp cayenne pepper
½ tsp smoked paprika
pink Himalayan salt
    or sea salt and
    freshly ground
    black pepper

1. Preheat the oven to 375°F/190°C.

2. Make the spice mix by combining all the spices in a small bowl with a pinch of salt and pepper. Keep the bowl to one side.

3. Place the sliced onions and peppers in a roasting pan, drizzle them with the olive oil, and add a pinch of salt and pepper. Roast the vegetables in the oven for 30–35 minutes, adding the mushrooms after 10 minutes.

4. Turn on the broiler.

5. Place the corn in a baking pan, about 6 inches under the broiler, and toast each side for 3–5 minutes, or until the kernels are nicely charred. Remove the pan from the oven and set it aside.

6. Place the rice in a saucepan. Cover it with water and bring it to a boil over medium-high heat. Turn the heat down to medium-low and cook the rice for 25 minutes, or according to the instructions on the package.

7. When the rice is cooked, drain any excess water and add the tomatoes with the spice mix and chopped chili. Return the pan to low heat for 5 minutes until warmed through. Stir in the roasted vegetables and transfer the mixture into a serving bowl.

8. Serve the rice mixture, sliced avocado, Summer Salsa, and Cashew Cheese wrapped in large lettuce leaves, with the corn on the side, and dig in!

INDONESIAN KEBABS + SATAY SAUCE

Serves 4

I make these kebabs frequently during the summer to take to barbecues on the beach in Brighton. The vibrant colors and taste of fresh vegetables with the delicious, zingy peanut satay sauce are a perfect pairing.

Ingredients

marinade
2 tbsp olive oil
1 tbsp lime juice
1 tbsp tamari
½ tsp ground cumin
pink Himalayan salt
    or sea salt and
    freshly ground
    black pepper

kebabs
10 button mushrooms
2 red or yellow bell
    peppers, seeded
    and chopped into
    ¾-inch chunks
1 zucchini, chopped
    into ¼-inch cubes
1 red onion, chopped
    into ¾-inch cubes
12 ripe cherry
    tomatoes
1 small eggplant,
    chopped into
    ¾-inch cubes

satay sauce
2 tsp sesame oil
1 shallot, peeled
    and diced
1 garlic clove, peeled
    and crushed
1 x 14-oz (400-g) can
    coconut milk
4 tbsp smooth
    peanut butter
1 tbsp tamari
2 tsp honey
juice of ½ lime

1. Make the marinade simply by mixing all the ingredients together in a large bowl with a pinch of salt and black pepper.

2. Toss the vegetables in the marinade, then cover with plastic wrap and refrigerate for 1 hour.

3. If you are using wooden skewers, soak them in water for 20 minutes so they don't burn during cooking. Preheat the oven to 350°F/180°C.

4. Thread the marinated vegetables onto metal or wooden skewers, alternating the vegetables each time.

5. Place the kebabs on a baking sheet, turning once or twice, until throughly cooked and nicely browned.

6. Meanwhile, to make the satay sauce, heat the sesame oil in a nonstick saucepan over medium heat. Fry the shallot for 6 minutes until softened, and add the garlic in the final minute, stirring occasionally.

7. Add the coconut milk with ¼ cup (60ml) water, the peanut butter, tamari, honey, lime juice, and chili flakes, and simmer for 3–5 minutes until thickened, stirring often. If you prefer a smoother consistency, process the mixture in a blender for a couple of minutes.

8. Serve the kebabs sprinkled with the chopped cilantro, chopped peanuts, and juice from the lime wedges. Serve the peanut satay sauce on the side for dipping.

a pinch of dried
    chili flakes
a small bunch of
    fresh cilantro,
    chopped, to serve
2 tbsp unsalted raw
    peanuts, chopped,
    to serve
1 lime, cut into
    wedges, to serve

Serving ideas ...
I serve these kebabs with a green salad and some sweet potato
wedges. They also go particularly well with my Avocado
+ Turmeric Salad with Quinoa (see page 77), as part
of a picnic spread.

CAULIFLOWER "STEAK" WITH CHIMICHURRI

Serves 4

You're probably thinking it's ridiculous calling this a steak, but when it is thickly sliced, cauliflower can be transformed into something very different from the vegetable you may be used to. It can be a great replacement for meat. The best accompaniment for it is my garlicky, herby chimichurri sauce, which originated in Argentina.

Ingredients

2 large heads of
  cauliflower
1 tbsp olive oil

chimichurri sauce
2 shallots, peeled
  and chopped
6 garlic cloves, peeled
  and chopped
½–1 fresh red chili,
  seeded and
  chopped
1 bunch of fresh
  parsley leaves,
  chopped
1 bunch of fresh
  cilanto, leaves
  chopped
½ cup (125ml)
  extra-virgin olive oil
4 tsp dried oregano
4 tbsp apple cider
  vinegar
juice of 1 lime
pink Himalayan salt
  or sea salt and
  freshly ground
  black pepper

1. Preheat the oven to 350°F/180°C.

2. To make the chimichurri sauce, simply place all the ingredients in a blender and process to make a rough paste, adding extra oil or water if needed.

3. Remove the outer leaves of the cauliflower and slice it lengthwise into ½-inch (1-cm) thick slices. Try to cut at least four whole steaks from each cauliflower.

4. Heat the oil in a large frying pan over high heat. Once hot, fry the cauliflower steaks for 1 minute on each side—you will need to do this in batches.

5. Transfer the cauliflower steaks to a baking pan and rub about 8 tablespoons of the chimichurri sauce over all the slices on each side. Bake the "steaks" for 25 minutes, or until they're cooked through, turning them halfway through the cooking time.

6. Serve with the remaining chimichurri sauce on top.

Tip ... Grate any pieces of cauliflower that have fallen off the slices and use them for Cauliflower Rice (see page 90).

Serving ideas ...
Serve the cauliflower steaks with a couple of your favorite side dishes—I always serve them with my Spiced Wedges (see page 150) and a salad.

MEDITERRANEAN MEZZE

I have traveled to the Greek Islands a few times, and one of my favorite things to eat there is the traditional mezze—a platter of various Greek dishes, including hummus, falafel, and dolmades. I created my own plant-based version back in rainy London.

BAKED FALAFEL

Serves 4 as part of a mezze

Ingredients

1 x 14-oz (400-g) can chickpeas, drained
3 garlic cloves, peeled and crushed
½ red onion, roughly chopped
1 tsp ground cumin
¼ bunch of fresh parsley,
    leaves picked
¼ bunch of fresh cilantro,
    leaves picked
1 tbsp tahini
1 tbsp sesame seeds
½ tsp paprika
¼ tsp dried chili flakes
coconut oil, for greasing
pink Himalayan salt or sea salt and
    freshly ground black pepper

1. Preheat the oven to 375°F/190°C.

2. Add all the ingredients to a food processor, with a pinch of salt and black pepper. Blend until the mixture holds together well, but is not entirely smooth, adding a tablespoon of water if needed.

3. Grease a baking sheet. Take heaping tablespoons of the mixture and form them into balls. Place them on the baking sheet and flatten them slighly. Bake for 30 minutes, turning the falafel halfway through.

COLLARD GREEN DOLMADES

Serves 4 as part of a mezze

Ingredients

½ cup (100g) brown rice, rinsed
1 tsp olive oil
½ onion, finely diced
2 garlic cloves, peeled and crushed
¼ red bell pepper, seeded and finely diced
a couple of sprigs each of fresh parsley,
    mint, and dill, finely chopped
4 unsulphured dried apricots,
    finely chopped
juice of 1 lemon
1 tbsp tahini
13 collard leaves
pink Himalayan salt or sea salt and
    freshly ground black pepper
extra-virgin olive oil, to serve

1. Place the rice in a saucepan, cover it with water, and bring to a boil over high heat. Turn the heat down to medium-low and simmer for 25 minutes or according to the package instructions.

2. Meanwhile, heat the olive oil in a frying pan over medium-high heat and fry the onion for 5–7 minutes until softened. Add the garlic and fry for a minute. Add the finely diced pepper and cook, stirring occasionally, for 7–10 minutes. Then remove from the heat and keep to one side.

3. Once the rice is cooked, stir in the pepper and onion mixture, herbs, apricots, lemon juice, and tahini. Season with salt and pepper and keep to one side.

4. Trim the thick stems off the collard leaves by cutting a triangular shape at the base of the stem, where it is thickest—this will make the leaves easier to roll.

5. Place a saucepan of boiling water over high heat, set a lidded steamer basket on top, and steam 10 of the leaves, one at a time, for about 45 seconds each until softened—you can do this as you wrap the dolmades rather than waiting until you have steamed all the leaves.

6. Take one steamed leaf and, with the vein side up, add a tablespoon of the rice mixture to the center. Fold it over once, tuck in each side, and roll up the leaf like a tortilla wrap. Repeat with the remaining 9 leaves.

7. Line the steamer basket with the 3 raw leaves—this will prevent the dolmades from sticking to the bottom. Place all the dolmades in the steamer on top of the leaves and steam for 15 minutes.

8. Allow the dolmades to cool and then refrigerate them for at least an hour. They taste even better after being in the fridge overnight! When ready to serve, drizzle the dolmades with a little bit of extra-virgin olive oil.

Tip ... Make this a full mezze by serving it with a few other dishes, such as my classic Hummus (see page 162) and my Greek Island Salad (see page 69).

VEGETABLE LAKSA

Serves 2

Although laksa originated in China, I first tried it in Indonesia and have since had it again in Singapore. Traditionally, this dish, which consists of noodles in a curry soup, does not have many vegetables, but of course I've loaded my version up with fresh produce. It's a perfect midweek meal.

Ingredients

paste
½ fresh red chili, seeded and sliced
2 garlic cloves, peeled and chopped
¾ to 1-inch piece of fresh ginger, peeled and chopped
2 shallots, peeled and chopped
juice of ½ lemon
2 tbsp tamari
a pinch of ground cloves
1 tsp coconut sugar
1 tsp turmeric

laksa
1 onion, diced
1 tsp coconut oil
1 red bell pepper, seeded and sliced
8 baby corn, halved lengthwise
about 20 sugar snap peas
½ x 14-oz (400-g) can coconut milk
4 oz (100g) brown rice udon or buckwheat noodles
a large handful of fresh cilantro leaves
2 small handfuls of bean sprouts, to serve
½ scallion, sliced, to serve
2 lime wedges, to serve

1. Start by making the laksa paste. Reserve a few slices of the chili for garnishing at the end, then blend all the ingredients for the paste in a blender until smooth. Set aside.

2. Fry the onion in the coconut oil for 5 minutes over medium heat, then add the laksa paste to the pan, and stir well.

3. Turn the heat up slightly, add the remaining vegetables, and fry for 3–5 minutes more, stirring occasionally.

4. Pour in 2 cups (500ml) water and the coconut milk. Bring to a boil. Add the noodles and simmer for 7 minutes or until the noodles are cooked.

5. Stir in half the cilantro. Serve in bowls with the lime wedges and sprinkle the bean sprouts, remaining cilantro, scallions, and chili slices on top.

Tip ... Use the leftover coconut milk in another recipe—try my Warming Squash Soup (see page 80).

MUSHROOM MISO HOT POT

Serves 4

A regular appearance on menus at Japanese restaurants is a hot pot of rice with a delicious variety of vegetables. Because I love this dish so much, I wanted to create a similar one that's easy to make at home with fresh and wholesome ingredients.

Ingredients

1½ cups (300g) brown
    short-grain rice
1½ cups (150g) mixed
    mushrooms, such
    as shiitake,
    oyster, and enoki,
    roughly chopped
1 leek, trimmed,
    sliced, and rinsed
1 tbsp miso paste
1 fresh red chili,
    seeded and
    finely sliced
1 tbsp tamari
1 tsp coconut sugar
½ x 14-oz (400-g)
    package firm tofu,
    cut into small cubes
1 tsp coconut oil
a handful of enoki
    mushrooms,
    to serve
1 scallion,
    trimmed and
    sliced, to serve

mushroom stock
2-inch piece of fresh
    ginger, peeled
    and chopped
2 garlic cloves, peeled
5 cremini mushrooms,
    sliced
pink Himalayan salt
    or sea salt and
    freshly ground
    black pepper

1. Make the mushroom stock by bringing 4 cups (1 liter) water to a boil with the ginger, garlic, mushrooms, and a pinch of salt and black pepper. Simmer for 15 minutes.

2. Add the rice, bring to a boil, stir in the mushrooms and leek, and simmer for 25 minutes, until cooked, adding more boiling water, if needed. Halfway through, stir in the miso paste, chili, tamari, and coconut sugar.

3. While the rice is cooking, put the tofu on a cutting board. Place another board and a heavy pan or plate on top to press the tofu down and remove excess water. Leave for about 20 minutes.

4. Once the tofu has been weighed down for 20 minutes, drain any liquid, pat the tofu dry with paper towels, and cut it into cubes.

5. Fry the tofu in the coconut oil in a frying pan over medium heat for 8–10 minutes until golden.

6. Once the rice is cooked, stir the tofu into the rice and serve in bowls, with the raw enoki mushrooms and sliced scallions on top.

━● Tip ... Use the extra tofu in my Spicy Asian Tofu Salad (see page 70) or Tofu Scramble (see page 62).

INDIAN DAL

Serves 2

Indian food is one of my favorite cuisines because I love anything spicy. This wonderful dal recipe is easy to make using ingredients that you probably already have in your pantry. High in protein and with so many wonderful, natural benefits that come from the spices, it's also incredibly good for you.

Ingredients

1 cup (250g) dried
    red lentils, rinsed
2 tsp cumin seeds
1 tsp mustard seeds
1 tsp coriander seeds
1 onion, peeled
    and diced
3-inch piece of
    fresh ginger, peeled
    and grated
3 garlic cloves,
    peeled and crushed
1 tbsp coconut oil
½ bunch of fresh
    cilantro, leaves
    picked and stalks
    finely chopped
1 tsp turmeric
½ tsp chili powder
pink Himalayan salt
    or sea salt
4 vine-ripened
    tomatoes, chopped

1. Soak the lentils in about 3 cups (750ml) water for at least 1 hour or ideally overnight.

2. Drain the lentils and cook them in 3 cups (750ml) water. Bring to a boil, then simmer over low heat for 15 minutes, until thickened and all the water has been absorbed.

3. Fry the cumin, mustard, and coriander seeds in a dry frying pan over medium heat for a few seconds. Remove the spices from the heat, lightly crush them in a mortar and pestle, then return them to the pan.

4. Grind the onion, ginger, and garlic into a paste using a mortar and pestle or a food processor.

5. Return the pan to medium heat. Add the coconut oil with the cilantro stalks, turmeric, chili powder, a pinch of salt, and the onion, ginger, and garlic paste. Fry for about 2 minutes.

6. Stir in the tomatoes and cook for another 10–15 minutes, until the tomatoes have softened. Mix in the cooked lentils and sprinkle with cilantro.

━━● Tip ... This dish and my Friday Night Curry (see page 127) make delicious and easy midweek meals. They taste even better the next day, so save a portion for lunch. Or you can cook both dishes and serve them together for a curry night for 4.

FRIDAY NIGHT CURRY

Serves 2

One of my favorite things to eat is curry, but it is often very high in sodium and unhealthy fats. I decided to create my own with all the flavor, but more goodness. I've served this curry with wild rice and chickpeas for the high fiber content, and the chickpeas also deliver a good protein punch.

Ingredients

1 cup (190g) wild rice, rinsed
1 tsp coconut oil
1 onion, finely diced
2 garlic cloves, peeled and crushed
2-inch piece of fresh ginger, peeled and grated
1 fresh red chili, seeded and finely chopped
1 red bell pepper, seeded and diced
1 x 14-oz (400-g) can chickpeas, drained
1 x 14-oz (400-g) can chopped tomatoes
a large handful of spinach
pink Himalayan salt or sea salt and freshly ground black pepper
¼ bunch of fresh cilantro, leaves picked, to serve
1 lemon, cut into wedges, to serve

spice mix
½ tsp chili powder
½ tsp garam masala
1 tsp ground cumin
1 tsp turmeric
1 tsp ground coriander

1. Cook the rice according to the package instructions.

2. Combine the spice mix ingredients in a small bowl.

3. Heat the coconut oil in a medium saucepan over medium heat and fry the diced onion for 5–7 minutes.

4. Add the garlic, ginger, and fresh red chili, to taste, to the pan and fry for a minute or two.

5. Now add the spice mix, bit by bit, with the diced pepper, chickpeas, and chopped tomatoes. Fill half the empty tomato can with water and add the water to the pan. Add more of the spice mixture to your taste. I tend to use all of it.

6. Place a lid on the saucepan and simmer for 10 minutes. Then remove the lid and simmer for 10 minutes more.

7. Once cooked, stir in the spinach. Season to taste with salt and pepper and serve with the rice, sprinkled with the cilantro leaves, and a wedge of lemon on the side.

SHEPHERD'S PIE

Serves 4

This is my ultimate comfort food, perfect for a winter night in. To get the "meaty" consistency here, I've combined mushrooms, walnuts, and lentils, which provide a wonderful taste and texture, topped with delicious parsnips and potatoes.

Ingredients

½ cup (100g) dried
  Puy lentils
1 onion, chopped
olive oil
1 garlic clove, peeled
  and chopped
2 carrots, peeled
  and diced
2 cups (200g) cremini
  mushrooms, diced
1 cup (100g) unsalted
  raw walnuts,
  finely chopped
1 cup (150g) peas
½ cup (125ml) red wine
  (optional)
½ organic low-sodium
  vegetable
  bouillon cube
1 tsp yeast extract
1 x 14-oz (400-g) can
  chopped tomatoes
1 tsp Italian seasoning

topping

4 parsnips, peeled
  and chopped
2 medium potatoes,
  peeled and
  chopped
1 cup (250ml)
  unsweetened
  almond milk
a couple of sprigs
  of fresh thyme,
  leaves picked
pink Himalayan salt
  or sea salt and
  freshly ground
  black pepper

1. Preheat the oven to 400°F/200°C. Start by cooking the lentils according to the package instructions.

2. While the lentils are cooking, cook the parsnips and potatoes for the topping. Place both in a saucepan, cover with cold water, bring to a boil, and cook for 20 minutes or until soft.

3. Meanwhile, set a large saucepan over medium-high heat and fry the onion in a little olive oil for 5 minutes until softened, stirring regularly.

4. Add the garlic, carrots, and mushrooms to the pan. Fry for a few more minutes, then remove from the heat, and set aside.

5. Once the lentils are cooked, drain and add them to the saucepan along with the walnuts and peas.

6. Pour ½ cup (125ml) boiling water into a mixing bowl, add the red wine, or replace with extra water (if not using), the bouillon cube, and yeast extract. Stir to dissolve the cube.

7. Pour the liquid into the pan along with the canned tomatoes and seasoning and stir. Bring the liquid to a boil, then turn the heat down to medium-low, and simmer for about 15 minutes.

8. When the parsnips and potatoes are cooked, drain and mash them until smooth. Mix in the almond milk and black pepper.

9. Transfer the cooked vegetables and lentils to a baking dish and evenly spoon over the parsnip and potato mash, right to the edges of the dish, using a fork to fluff up the mash.

10. Toss the thyme in the olive oil, sprinkle it over the mashed potato and parsnip, and bake for 30 minutes or until golden.

ITALIAN STUFFED PEPPERS

Serves 4

When I went to a fine Italian restaurant at the Four Seasons, in Mauritius of all places, I ate a traditional stuffed pepper. It wasn't the healthiest, but I loved it so much, I decided to make my own version with brown rice, an abundance of vegetables, and crunchy pine nuts.

Ingredients

1 cup (200g) brown rice
4 large red bell peppers
2 tbsp olive oil
2 tsp coconut oil
4 garlic cloves, peeled and finely sliced
8 oz (225g) green beans, trimmed and cut into ¼-inch pieces
4 tsp capers, roughly chopped
½ cup (50g) sun-dried tomatoes in oil, drained and sliced
6 tbsp pine nuts
2 tbsp apple cider vinegar
2 tbsp nutritional yeast
2 tsp dried basil
pink Himalayan salt or sea salt and freshly ground black pepper
8 fresh basil leaves, to serve

1. Preheat the oven to 350°F/ 180°C.

2. Place the rice in a saucepan, cover with water, and bring to a boil over medium-high heat. Turn the heat down to medium-low and cook for 25 minutes, or according to the package instructions, until cooked through.

3. When the rice is almost cooked, slice the peppers straight down the middle lengthwise, keeping the stalks intact. Remove the seeds, place the peppers in a large baking pan, drizzle with the olive oil, and roast in the oven for 10–15 minutes.

4. Meanwhile, heat the coconut oil in a large frying pan over medium heat. Add the garlic, green beans, capers, and sun-dried tomatoes. Cook for 3–4 minutes, stirring regularly.

5. Remove the pan from the heat, add the remaining ingredients, reserving a few pine nuts, and drain. Add the cooked rice, stirring to combine.

6. Remove the peppers from the oven, stuff with the rice filling, sprinkle with the reserved pine nuts, place back in the oven, and roast for 20–25 minutes. Serve with fresh basil leaves on top.

BULGUR WHEAT STUFFED ZUCCHINIS

Serves 4

I first created this recipe when I had friends over for dinner. I had been out all day and got back late, so I didn't have time to make anything fancy—I put this together in 30 minutes and they loved it! Bulgur has a wonderful texture and absorbs the delicious flavors of the vegetables.

Ingredients

4 large zucchinis
1 tbsp coconut oil,
    plus extra for
    the zucchinis
1 ear of corn, husked
1 cup (160g) bulgur
    wheat, rinsed
1 organic low-sodium
    vegetable bouillon
    cube
1 onion, diced
1 red bell pepper,
    seeded
    and diced
5 cremini mushrooms,
    finely sliced
2 garlic cloves, peeled
    and finely chopped
½ fresh red chili,
    seeded and
    finely chopped
1 tsp Cajun seasoning
1 tsp smoked paprika
1 tbsp apple cider
    vinegar
1 x Tomato Sauce
    recipe (see
    page 109)
pink Himalayan salt
    or sea salt and
    freshly ground
    black pepper

1. Preheat the oven to 350°F/180°C.

2. Halve the zucchinis lengthwise and scoop out the seeds. Rub with a little coconut oil, place in a baking pan, and bake in the oven for 15–20 minutes, turning halfway through the cooking.

3. Boil the corn in a saucepan for 3–5 minutes, then remove it from the pan, and set it aside. Reserve 2 cups (500ml) water in the saucepan. Once the corn cools, slice off the kernels.

4. Dissolve the bouillon cube in the reserved water. Stir in the bulgur wheat and cook over medium heat for 15 minutes, then drain, and set aside.

5. Heat 1 tablespoon coconut oil in a frying pan over medium heat and fry the onion for 5 minutes. Add all the remaining vegetables, garlic, chili, and seasoning. Season well with salt and black pepper and fry for about 8 minutes.

6. Stir in the cooked bulgur wheat with the apple cider vinegar and spoon the mixture into each of the zucchini halves.

7. Bake for an additional 5 minutes, then serve with the tomato sauce, and the remaining bulgur wheat on the side.

"CHEESY" BAKED PASTA

Serves 4

When I was a teenager, my speciality was baked pasta. Back then, I added canned tuna, cheese, and butter, but now, being on a plant-based diet, I have adapted my original comfort food to make it nourishing and feature more sophisticated flavors. This is great to serve with a slice of garlic bread.

Ingredients

1 zucchini, chopped
1 red bell pepper,
    seeded
    and sliced
1 orange bell pepper,
    seeded
    and sliced
1 onion, sliced
1 tbsp olive oil
3¼ cups (250g)
    brown rice pasta
1 large vine-ripened
    tomato, sliced
pink Himalayan salt
    or sea salt and
    freshly ground
    black pepper
2 tbsp pine nuts,
    to serve
a small handful of
    fresh basil leaves,
    chopped, to serve

spicy tomato sauce
1 garlic clove, peeled
    and crushed
1 tbsp olive oil
2 x 14-oz (400-g) cans
    chopped tomatoes
2 tbsp tomato purée
1 tbsp Italian
    seasoning
½ tsp dried chili flakes
2 tbsp capers

1. Preheat the oven to 400°F/200°C.

2. Place the vegetables in a roasting pan with a drizzle of olive oil and roast for 25 minutes.

3. Cook the pasta with a pinch of salt according to the package instructions, then drain, and set aside.

4. While the vegetables are roasting and the pasta is cooking, make the tomato sauce. Fry the garlic with the olive oil in a large saucepan over medium-high heat for a few seconds, until fragrant. Add the remaining ingredients, turn the heat down to low, and simmer for 15 minutes.

5. To make the "cheese" sauce, heat the coconut oil in a small saucepan over medium heat. Add the diced shallot and fry for 5–7 minutes to soften before adding the garlic and frying for another minute. Add 1 tablespoon of the flour and use a whisk to stir it in. Add the remaining flour, whisking constantly. Then slowly mix in the almond milk, bit by bit.

6. Once the flour has dissolved into the almond milk, add the remaining sauce ingredients. Continue to use the whisk to make sure there are no lumps, and then keep the mixture on very low heat, stirring frequently.

7. When the roasted vegetables are cooked, remove them from the oven and turn the heat down to 350°F/180°C.

"cheese" sauce
2 tsp coconut oil
1 shallot, peeled
   and diced
2 garlic cloves, peeled
   and crushed
2 tbsp buckwheat flour
1 cup (250ml)
   unsweetened
   almond milk
2 tbsp nutritional yeast
1 tbsp apple cider
   vinegar

garlic bread
8 garlic cloves, peeled
   and crushed
4 thick slices of rye or
   sourdough bread
4 tsp dried
   Italian seasoning
extra-virgin olive oil
a handful of fresh
   basil leaves,
   chopped

8. Stir the roasted vegetables and cooked pasta into the tomato sauce. Put the pasta mixture into an 8 x 12 inch baking pan, pour the "cheese" sauce on top, and smooth down the sauce with a spoon. Add the sliced tomato to the top and bake for 30 minutes.

9. Lightly toast the pine nuts in a dry frying pan over medium heat and set aside.

10. To make the garlic bread, turn on the broiler. Rub the crushed garlic onto one side of each slice of bread, sprinkle with Italian seasoning, and drizzle with olive oil. Toast for 5 minutes under the broiler, or until golden, then sprinkle with the basil.

11. Serve the pasta sprinkled with the toasted pine nuts and chopped basil on top, along with the garlic bread.

MACARONI AND "CHEESE" WITH ROASTED TOMATOES

Serves 2

My family has a recipe for a creamy, cheesy pasta dish with tomatoes. Obviously, it's not the healthiest, so I set myself the challenge to see if I could make a creamy, but plant-based, pasta dish. This exceeded my expectations and is now one of my favorite curl-up-on-the-sofa dinners. Get a head start by soaking the cashews overnight.

Ingredients

6 ripe cherry
    tomatoes, halved
1 tsp olive oil
a pinch of dried
    thyme
2 cups (200g) brown
    rice macaroni pasta
pink Himalayan salt
    or sea salt and
    freshly ground
    black pepper

"cheese" sauce
¼ small butternut
    squash (approx.
    8 oz), peeled
    and chopped
½ small onion, diced
½ tsp coconut oil
1 garlic clove, peeled
    and diced
¼ cup (40g) unsalted
    raw cashews,
    soaked overnight
½ cup (125ml) brown
    rice milk or other
    non-dairy milk
2 tbsp nutritional yeast
½ tsp whole grain
    mustard
a pinch of ground
    nutmeg
juice of ½ lemon

1. Preheat the oven to 375°F/190°C.

2. For the "cheese" sauce, place a saucepan of boiling water over high heat. Set a lidded steamer basket on top and steam the squash for 15 minutes until soft.

3. Meanwhile, place the tomato halves on a baking pan lined with tin foil. Drizzle with the olive oil, a sprinkle of dried thyme, and a pinch of salt and pepper. Roast for 10–15 minutes.

4. Cook the pasta according to the instructions, drain, and rinse with cold water. Put the pasta back in the pan and set aside.

5. Place a frying pan over medium heat and fry the onion for the "cheese" sauce in the coconut oil for 5 minutes. Then add the garlic and continue to fry for another minute.

6. Drain the soaked cashews. Add the cashews, the steamed butternut squash, cooked onion and garlic, and the remaining sauce ingredients to a food processor. Blend until totally smooth.

7. Stir the "cheese" sauce into the cooked pasta and heat it over low heat for about 5 minutes. Serve in bowls with the roasted tomatoes on top.

Serves 4

For Christmas, I wanted to make a plant-based alternative to beef Wellington and the result was outstanding! What is essentially a nut roast made from lentils, vegetables, and nuts is then wrapped in thin eggplant slices. This is great for Sunday dinner, too, with roasted vegetables, mint sauce, and vegetable gravy.

Ingredients

mint sauce
3 bunches of fresh mint leaves
¼ cup (60ml) apple cider vinegar
pink Himalayan salt or sea salt and freshly ground black pepper

nut Wellington
½ cup (125g) red split lentils
1 onion, diced
1 tsp coconut oil, plus extra for the eggplants
5 cremini mushrooms, chopped
1 carrot, peeled and chopped
1 red bell pepper, seeded and chopped
2 garlic cloves, peeled and diced
1 tsp dried thyme
1 tsp dried rosemary
5 sage leaves, chopped
1 tsp apple cider vinegar

1. To make the mint sauce, sprinkle a good pinch of salt onto the mint leaves. Chop them finely and add them to a bowl or jar.

2. Stir in the apple cider vinegar and a pinch of freshly ground pepper. Pour over ¼ cup (60ml) boiling water and stir.

3. Allow the sauce to cool, then refrigerate it for at least 1 hour, but preferably overnight, for the flavors to infuse. Refrigerate in an airtight jar or container.

4. Preheat the oven to 375°F/190°C.

5. Add the lentils to a saucepan with 1 cup of water. Bring the water to a boil and simmer for 15–20 minutes or until the lentils are cooked.

6. Set a frying pan over medium-high heat and fry the onion in the coconut oil for 5–7 minutes. Add the remaining vegetables and garlic, except for the eggplants, and continue to fry for 10–15 minutes, until the vegetables have softened.

7. Stir in the herbs and apple cider vinegar. Season well with a pinch of salt and pepper.

8. In a food processor, pulse the mixed nuts into small chunks. Add the cooked lentils and the vegetables. Blend until everything is combined, but small chunks remain. Set aside.

(recipe continues on the next page)

1 cup (125g) mixed
nuts, such as
Brazil, cashew,
walnuts, chopped
2 large eggplants
pink Himalayan salt
or sea salt and
freshly ground
black pepper

9. Cut the stalks off the eggplants and cut them into wide, flat ¼-inch (2-mm) thick slices. Some slices won't come out right, but that's why the recipe calls for 2 eggplants, to allow room for error.

10. Place the eggplant slices on a large baking sheet, rub with coconut oil, and bake for 10–15 minutes, turning the slices halfway through the cooking time.

11. Lightly grease an 8 x 4-inch (20 x 10-cm) loaf pan with coconut oil and place the eggplant slices around the sides of the pan, keeping them high enough so that the tops of the slices will overlap and cover the top of the nutloaf. Lay the eggplant slices along the base so the entire inside of the loaf pan is covered.

12. Pour in the Wellington mixture, using a wooden spoon to pack it in and smooth the top. Then place a single layer of eggplant slices on top. Fold over the top of the eggplant slices lining the side of the pan so that they cover the top of the loaf. Use toothpicks to keep the slices in place.

13. Bake the roast on the middle rack of the oven for 40 minutes. Remove the pan and allow it to cool slightly. To remove the roast from the pan, pull out the toothpicks, and place a cutting board on top of the pan. Then flip it over and gently lift off the pan.

14. Slice the nut roast into four equal portions and serve it with the mint sauce.

🥣 Serving ideas ...
Roasted Carrots with Thyme (see page 153).
Roasted Brussels Sprouts with Garlic (see page 153).
Rosemary-roasted Sweet Potatoes (see page 150).

🥄 Tip ... Slice any leftover eggplant into chunks and use it in my Quick Quinoa (see page 142).

CREAMY LEEK + CELERY ROOT PIE

Serves 4

Eating a hearty pie with a crisp crust and a smooth, creamy filling—who would've thought this could be possible on a plant-based diet? Well, I've made it possible with this absolute showstopper of a main meal. Bring this to a table of hungry family members, and they will not be disappointed. Get a head start by soaking the cashews overnight.

Ingredients

1 small celery root, peeled and chopped
olive oil
4 leeks, trimmed and sliced
1 whole broccoli, broken into small florets

sauce
1 cup (150g) unsalted raw cashews, soaked overnight
2¼ cups (300ml) oat milk
1 tsp whole grain mustard
1 tbsp nutritional yeast
1 garlic clove, peeled
a handful of fresh chives, chopped
pink Himalayan salt or sea salt and freshly ground black pepper

pie crust
1 tbsp milled flaxseed
1 cup (150g) whole-wheat flour
1 cup (150g) spelt flour
¼ tsp salt
¼ cup (60ml) olive oil

1. Preheat the oven to 350°F/180°C.

2. Place the celery root in a roasting pan, drizzle with olive oil, and roast for 30 minutes.

3. After the 30 minutes is up, add the leeks to the celery root and roast for another 15 minutes.

4. Make the sauce by draining the cashews and blending them in a food processor until they are broken apart. Then add the remaining ingredients, except for the chives, with a pinch of salt and black pepper, and blend on full power for about 3 minutes until totally smooth.

5. Stir in the chopped chives and set the mixture aside while you make the pie crust.

6. Mix the flaxseed with 2 tablespoons of water and set it aside.

7. In a large bowl, combine both the flours and pie salt. Then add the olive oil and ⅓ cup (90ml) cold water, plus more if needed, and mix together. Once thickened, add the flaxseed mixture to the bowl and use your hands to fully combine the mixture, until it all comes together.

8. Roll the dough on a lightly floured surface unti it is ¼-inch thick and about 3-inches wider than the diameter of your pie pan.

9. Combine the roasted vegetables with the broccoli and the sauce to make the filling. Spoon it into the pie pan.

10. Carefully drape the pastry over the pie pan. Use your thumb and forefinger to crimp and seal the pastry edges around the rim. Using a sharp knife, make a small cross in the center of the pie crust.

11. Bake for 40–45 minutes until cooked through.

QUICK QUINOA

Serves 2

I created this recipe when I had my close friend Tanya for dinner one evening, and I needed to make something tasty in about 30 minutes. Luckily, quinoa is really quick, so I cooked it with a variety of fresh vegetables, spices, sweet dates, and pomegranate. It was a treat!

Ingredients

1 cup (200g)
    quinoa, rinsed
1 tbsp coconut oil
1 red onion, diced
½ tsp turmeric
½ tsp ground
    cinnamon
1 tsp ground cumin
1 eggplant, cubed
10 ripe cherry
    tomatoes,
    quartered
1 yellow bell pepper,
    seeded and diced
1 x 14-oz (400-g) can
    chopped tomatoes
½ fresh red chill,
    seeded and diced
2 Medjool dates,
    pitted and diced
a large handful
    of spinach
½ pomegranate,
    seeded
a bunch of fresh
    cilantro, leaves
    picked and
    chopped
pink Himalayan salt
    or sea salt and
    freshly ground
    black pepper

1. Put the quinoa in a saucepan with 2 cups (500ml) of water. Place the pan over medium heat, bring the water to a boil, then turn the heat down to low, and simmer for 15 minutes until the water has been absorbed and the quinoa is cooked, adding more water if needed. Keep to one side.

2. Heat half of the coconut oil in a frying pan over medium heat, add the onion, and fry for 5 minutes until softened.

3. Add the spices, fry for a couple more minutes, then add the eggplant, and fry it for about 10 minutes, until softened, adding more coconut oil if needed.

4. Add the cherry tomatoes and pepper with a pinch of salt and black pepper. Fry for 5 more minutes.

5. Add the canned tomatoes, chili, and dates. Bring to a simmer.

6. Remove the mixture from the heat, stir in the spinach and quinoa, and serve sprinkled with the pomegranate seeds and the chopped cilantro.

Tip ... Save any leftover pomegranate seeds and sprinkle them over a bowl of homemade Muesli (see page 48) for breakfast.

ITALIAN FARRO + BEAN STEW

Serves 4

Whenever I think of stews, I'm reminded of my great grandmother, who made them for the whole family, usually with beef and dumplings. I used to love stews as a kid, so I wanted to create a healthier version that I can enjoy now—and this is the delicious result.

Ingredients

olive oil
1 onion, diced
2 carrots, peeled and diced
1 organic low-sodium vegetable bouillon cube
½ cup (50g) farro, rinsed
½ fresh red chili, peeled and chopped
1 garlic clove, peeled and diced
1 x 14-oz (400-g) can chopped tomatoes
1 x 14-oz (400-g) can cannellini beans, drained
1 lemon
2 tbsp nutritional yeast (optional)
3 packed cups (150g) spinach
½ bunch of fresh basil leaves, chopped
pink Himalayan salt or sea salt and freshly ground black pepper

1. Heat a little olive oil in a large saucepan over medium heat. Add the onion and fry it for 5 minutes until softened, stirring occasionally, then add the carrot, and fry for another 3 minutes.

2. Dissolve the bouillon cube in 3 cups (750ml) boiling water in a mixing bowl and keep to one side.

3. Add the farro, chili, and garlic to the carrots and fry for a an additional minute, stirring regularly, before adding the stock and chopped tomatoes.

4. Bring the mixture to a boil, then turn the heat down to medium-low, and simmer, stirring occasionally, for 30 minutes.

5. After 30 minutes, stir in the beans, squeeze in the lemon juice, add the nutritional yeast, if using, and simmer for 5 minutes more to warm through.

6. Season to taste with salt and pepper and, just before serving, stir in the spinach until wilted. Serve sprinkled with the basil.

Tip ... Make this recipe and freeze any leftover portions to defrost and eat another day.

SPRING GARDEN RISOTTO

Serves 4

When I first started cooking, I used to avoid making risotto because I thought it was too complicated, with the constant stirring and watching, but when I tried it out one day, I realized how easy it can be. I love the taste of spring from the wonderful greens in this dish.

Ingredients

1 organic low-sodium vegetable bouillon cube
2 shallots, peeled and diced
1 tbsp olive oil
juice of 1 lemon
1½ cups (300g) brown risotto rice or arborio rice
1 carrot, peeled and diced
½ zucchini, diced
¼ cup (175g) fresh, frozen, or canned fava beans
½ cup (80g) frozen peas
a small bunch of asparagus, woody ends removed and thinly sliced
2 scallions, trimmed and finely sliced
1 tbsp nutritional yeast
¼ bunch of fresh mint, leaves picked and chopped
pink Himalayan salt or sea salt and freshly ground black pepper
a handful of watercress, to serve

1. Dissolve the bouillon cube in 6 cups (1.5 liters) boiling water in a saucepan over low heat.

2. Place a frying pan over medium-low heat and fry the shallots in the olive oil for 5 minutes until softened. Add half the lemon juice and the rice and fry for another 2 minutes.

3. Add the carrot with the remaining lemon juice and fry for 3–5 minutes.

4. Add one ladle of the vegetable stock to the pan and keep stirring until the rice has absorbed all the liquid. Repeat this for 25 minutes or according to the package instructions, adding one ladle of stock at a time and continuously stirring.

5. In the final 10 minutes, add the zucchini, fava beans, peas, asparagus, and scallions. When the last of the stock has been absorbed, season well with salt and pepper and remove from the heat. Stir in the nutritional yeast and most of the mint.

6. Serve sprinkled with the remaining mint and a handful of watercress on top.

Sides + Snacks

04

ROASTED MEDITERRANEAN VEGETABLES
Serves 4

I spent a lot of my childhood in Mallorca and loved the way the abundant local vegetables were used. These two recipes call for simply roasting a variety of vegetables to make tasty side dishes. I first discovered roasting whole garlic at a restaurant called The Stinking Rose in L.A., where everything includes garlic. My kind of restaurant! I love this spread on crackers.

SPANISH-STYLE

Serves 4

Ingredients

1 red bell pepper, seeded
1 yellow bell pepper, seeded
2 red onions
2 zucchinis
2 garlic cloves, unpeeled
1 tbsp coconut oil or olive oil
1 cup (125g) cherry tomatoes
1 tsp Italian seasoning
pink Himalayan salt or sea salt
   and freshly ground black pepper

1. Preheat the oven to 375°F/190°C.

2. Slice the peppers and onions into strips and the zucchinis into discs. Cut the garlic cloves in half.

3. If you're using coconut oil, place it in a large roasting pan in the oven until it melts, before adding the vegetables.

4. Scatter the mixed herbs over the vegetables and make sure everything is evenly covered in the oil, then season with salt and black pepper. Roast the vegetables in the oven for 45 minutes, checking every 15 minutes that the vegetables are cooking evenly and not burning.

WHOLE ROASTED GARLIC

Serves 4

Ingredients

1 large whole garlic bulb
olive oil
rye bread or crackers,
   to serve

1. Preheat the oven to 375°F/190°C.

2. Remove the loose outer layers of the garlic and cut off the top— enough to expose the tops of the individual cloves.

3. Place the garlic on a sheet of tin foil and drizzle with olive oil. Wrap the garlic in the foil and roast it in the oven for 45 minutes.

4. To serve, spread the soft, roasted garlic on rye bread, crackers, or Rosemary Crackers (see page 166).

SWEET POTATOES

Serves 4

Sweet potato is probably my favorite vegetable, and when I first made these wedges I became a little obsessed! They are perfect dipped into Homemade Ketchup (see page 154) and are a lunchtime staple. Rosemary-roasted sweet potatoes are a great alternative to traditional roasted spuds.

SPICED WEDGES

Serves 4

Ingredients

2–3 sweet potatoes (approx. 28 oz/800g)
olive oil
1 tbsp Cajun spice
pink Himalayan salt or sea salt and
   freshly ground black pepper

1. Preheat the oven to 350°F/180°C.

2. Cut the sweet potatoes into wedges, trying to keep all the wedges the same size so they cook evenly.

3. Place the sweet potato wedges in a large roasting pan, drizzle over some olive oil, and sprinkle with the spice and seasoning. Mix them up with your hands or a spatula to make sure all the wedges are evenly covered and make sure they don't overlap in the pan.

4. Roast the sweet potatoes in the oven for 1 hour, turning them while they cook. Check on them occasionally, to make sure they don't overcook.

— Tip ... Try swapping out the Cajun spice for 1 teaspoon smoked paprika and 1 teaspoon dried mixed herbs for a different twist.

ROSEMARY-ROASTED

Serves 4

Ingredients

2 large sweet potatoes, peeled and
   chopped into 1½ inch (4cm) chunks
2 tbsp coconut oil
2 tbsp nutritional yeast
6 sprigs of fresh rosemary
   (3 whole, 3 with leaves picked)
pink Himalayan salt or sea salt and
   freshly ground black pepper

1. Preheat the oven to 375°F/190°C. Cover the sweet potatoes with water in a large saucepan. Bring to a boil and simmer for 8 minutes, then drain.

2. Add 1 tablespoon of the oil, along with a pinch of salt, pepper, and the nutritional yeast to the saucepan. Place the lid on the pan and gently shake it to fluff up the potatoes. This will give them a crispier finish.

3. Add the remaining coconut oil to a roasting pan and place it in the oven for a few seconds to melt. Then add the potatoes and whole rosemary sprigs to the pan and season with salt and pepper. Scatter over the rosemary leaves. Roast the sweet potatoes for 45–50 minutes, until they're nicely browned. Remove the rosemary sprigs before serving.

SUNDAY-LUNCH SIDES

Sunday lunch can be a rather monumental time for food, often involving vegetables roasted in lots of butter or oil. I use coconut oil to roast veggies, which gives them a wonderful crispness and mild taste. I serve them with my Nut Wellington (see page 137).

ROASTED CARROTS WITH THYME

Serves 4

Ingredients

1 tbsp coconut oil
6 fresh thyme sprigs
12 long, thin carrots, peeled and halved
   lengthwise, leafy tops intact
pink Himalayan salt or sea salt and
   freshly ground black pepper

1. Preheat the oven to 375°F/190°C.

2. While the oven is warming, put the coconut oil in a roasting pan and place it in the oven to melt.

3. Pick off and roughly chop half the thyme leaves. Place the carrots in the roasting pan with the 3 whole thyme sprigs, the chopped thyme, and a pinch of salt and black pepper.

4. Toss everything together in the coconut oil, making sure all the carrots are evenly covered, and roast them in the oven for 35–40 minutes, until they're cooked through and golden, turning them over halfway.

ROASTED BRUSSELS SPROUTS WITH GARLIC

Serves 4

Ingredients

1 tbsp coconut oil
3 large handfuls of
   Brussels sprouts (about 20)
4 garlic cloves, peeled and finely sliced
pink Himalayan salt or sea salt and
   freshly ground black pepper

1. Preheat the oven to 375°F/190°C.

2. While the oven is warming, add the coconut oil to a roasting pan and place it in the oven. Remove it when the oil has melted and set it aside.

3. Rinse and dry the Brussels sprouts, slice off the stems, and cut the sprouts in half. Add them to the roasting pan with salt and pepper, making sure the Brussels sprouts are fully covered, and roast them for 10 minutes.

4. Add the garlic cloves to the roasting pan and roast for 10 more minutes.

HOMEMADE TOMATO KETCHUP

Ketchup is one of those things that most people automatically buy at the supermarket and don't consider making at home, but it tastes so much fresher, of course, and doesn't contain lots of added sugar, if you make it yourself. Ketchup is easy to make and any leftovers can be used as a pasta sauce.

Ingredients

1 tsp coconut oil
2 shallots, peeled
    and finely diced
1 garlic clove, peeled
    and crushed
5 large vine-ripe
    tomatoes,
    roughly chopped
1 tsp honey
    (or other
    sweetener)
1 tbsp apple
    cider vinegar
½ tsp ground
    cinnamon
½ tsp dried basil

1. Add the coconut oil to a medium saucepan and fry the shallots and garlic over medium-high heat, stirring often.

2. Add the chopped tomatoes to the saucepan, then turn the heat down to low and cook for 7–10 minutes, until the tomatoes start to break down and soften. Stir the mixture to make sure it doesn't burn.

3. Add the remaining ingredients and use a wooden spoon to mash the tomatoes.

4. Simmer the tomato mixture for 15 minutes, then remove it from the heat and set it aside to cool.

5. Transfer the mixture to a blender and blend until smooth. Keep the ketchup in the fridge in an airtight container for 2–3 days.

ESSENTIAL SIDES

The dips on this page are inspired by Mexican cuisine, using red chilis and fresh cilantro. They're refreshing, zingy, slightly spicy, and work perfectly when paired together. The salsa will keep in the fridge, but the guacamole should be made just before you eat it, as the avocado will turn brown. Pesto is a versatile staple and I serve the cashew "cheese" with almost anything. It's so delicious, especially if you soak the cashews overnight, which gives the cheese a super smooth consistency.

SUMMER SALSA

Ingredients

2 cups (250g) vine-ripened
    cherry tomatoes
¼ red onion
juice of ½ lime
1 tbsp extra-virgin olive oil
½ fresh red chilis, seeded
a handful of fresh cilantro leaves
¼ cucumber, seeded and
    chopped into small chunks
pink Himalayan salt or sea salt and
    freshly ground black pepper

1. Place the tomatoes, onion, lime juice, olive oil, chili, and seasoning into a food processor and pulse until the tomatoes and onion are chopped to the desired consistency. Spoon out any excess liquid from the tomatoes.

2. Stir the cilantro into the salsa with the cucumber chunks.

➤ Tip ... If you don't have a food processor, just use a good knife to chop up the ingredients.

🥣 Serving ideas ...
Mexican Chili Bowl (see page 99).

GUACAMOLE

Ingredients

1 ripe avocado, peeled and pitted
5 vine-ripened cherry tomatoes
½ fresh red chili, seeded
juice of ½ lime
¼ bunch of fresh cilantro,
    stems removed
pink Himalayan salt or sea salt and
    freshly ground black pepper

1. Use the back of a fork to mash the avocado and set it aside.

2. Quarter the tomatoes and slice the chili. Stir them into the mashed avocado with the remaining ingredients. Serve immediately.

BASIL PESTO

Ingredients

a large bunch of fresh basil,
    stems removed
½ cup (60g) pumpkin seeds
½ cup (80g) pine nuts,
    plus 1 tbsp extra
juice of ½ lemon
2 garlic cloves, peeled
2 tbsp nutritional yeast
¼ cup (60ml) olive oil
pink Himalayan salt or sea salt and
    freshly ground black pepper

1. Place all the ingredients, except for
   a few basil leaves, into a blender or
   food processor, with a pinch of salt
   and black pepper, and process until
   smooth.

Tip ... Once you've made this
recipe, you can experiment with
different combinations of nuts and
herbs, such as walnuts, almonds, Brazil
nuts, and cashews. You can even
substitute the herbs with
parsley or cilantro.

Serving ideas ...
Stir the pesto into squash spaghetti and
top it with toasted seeds and fresh basil.
Toss a salad with the pesto or use it as a
salad dressing.

CASHEW "CHEESE"

Ingredients

1 cup (150g) unsalted raw cashews,
    soaked overnight
1 garlic clove, peeled and chopped
2 tbsp lemon juice
3 tbsp nutritional yeast
pink Himalayan salt or sea salt and
    freshly ground black pepper

1. Drain the cashews and place them
   in a food processor with ¼ cup
   (125ml) of water and the remaining
   ingredients.

2. Pulse the mixture until the cashews
   break down. Then blend for a couple
   more minutes until the cashew
   mixture is smooth. Season to taste.

ROOT CHIPS

If you're tempted by the bag of potato chips you've hidden in the kitchen, rustle up some of these root chips instead. You may not think they'll satisfy your craving for your favorite brand, but these bright, beautiful veggie chips taste incredible. They're also surprisingly quick and easy to whip up!

Ingredients

3–5 root vegetables, such as sweet potato, purple potato, white potato, carrot, parsnip, or red beet
1 tbsp olive oil
pink Himalayan salt or sea salt

Flavor options

1 tsp dried mixed herbs, smoked paprika, dried chili flakes, ground cumin, dried thyme, dried rosemary

1. Preheat the oven to 310°F/160°C.

2. Using the slicing side of a box grater, finely slice all the vegetables. Alternatively, you can finely slice them by hand or in a food processor.

3. Pat the vegetable slices dry on paper towels, then add them to a large bowl with the olive oil, salt, and your favorite flavorings (see ingredients list for my favorites). Mix with your hands until they're evenly coated, and then transfer them to baking sheets. Make sure the veggie slices are spaced evenly and don't overlap.

4. Cook the chips in the oven for 20–25 minutes until they're golden and crispy. Some may cook more quickly than others, so keep an eye on them. Remove the chips from the oven and allow them to cool.

🥣 Serving ideas ...

Try these chips with a selection of my dips (see pages 162–3).

HUMMUS—3 WAYS

I can quite proudly confess that I am a dip addict! The dips below can be enjoyed with crackers, vegetable crudités, or a salad. As I'm such a huge hummus fan, I've created three delicious, but very different, flavors.

CLASSIC

Ingredients

1 x 14-oz (400-g) can chickpeas, drained
2 garlic cloves, peeled
juice of 1 lemon
3 tbsp tahini
1 tsp ground cumin
3 tbsp extra-virgin olive oil, plus
    extra to serve
pink Himalayan salt or sea salt and
    freshly ground black pepper

1. Pulse the chickpeas and garlic cloves together for 1 minute in a food processor, then add the rest of the ingredients, along with a pinch of salt and pepper and a splash of water. Process until smooth. Serve with a drizzle of extra-virgin olive oil.

PINK BEET

Ingredients

1 x 14-oz (400-g) can chickpeas, drained
2 garlic cloves, peeled
1 red beet, roughly chopped
juice of 1 lemon
2 tbsp tahini
3 tbsp extra-virgin olive oil
pink Himalayan salt or sea salt and
    freshly ground black pepper

1. Pulse the chickpeas and garlic cloves for 1 minute in a food processor, then add the rest of the ingredients, with a pinch of salt and pepper, and a splash of water. Process until smooth.

PEA + MINT

Ingredients

2 cups (300g) peas, fresh or frozen
2 scallions, trimmed
10 fresh mint leaves
2 tbsp tahini
1 tbsp extra-virgin olive oil
zest and juice of ½ lemon
pink Himalayan salt or sea salt and
    freshly ground black pepper

1. Cook the peas in a saucepan of boiling water for about 3 minutes, then drain the peas.

2. Finely slice one half of a scallion and set it aside for a garnish.

3. Add the peas to a food processor with the remaining scallions, the mint, a splash of water, the tahini, olive oil, and lemon juice.

4. Process the mixture to the desired consistency. (I like it to be quite chunky.)

5. Keep the dip in the fridge until you're ready to use it, then sprinkle it with the lemon zest and reserved scallion slices.

DIPS

The nutritional yeast in my Sun-dried Tomato + Cashew dip gives it a cheesy flavor, but is totally optional. Spread the dip over a portobello mushroom and grill it for a few minutes, stir into a pasta, or simply add it to any dish as a light and delicious side. You can stir the hemp seeds into the cashew dip after blending, if you like (they'll almost pop in your mouth!). The Black Bean dip makes a great side to any Mexican dish—try it with my Mexican Chili Bowl (see page 99).

BLACK BEAN

Ingredients

2 x 14-oz (400-g) cans black beans, drained
juice of 1 lime
1 garlic clove, peeled and crushed
a small bunch of cilantro
2 tsp ground cumin
½ tsp dried chili flakes
1 tsp smoked paprika
2–3 tbsp canned coconut milk
pink Himalayan salt or sea salt and
    freshly ground black pepper

1. Add all the ingredients to a large bowl with a pinch of salt and pepper. Use a potato masher or a food processor to blend it all together. The dip doesn't have to be totally smooth. It can have some texture!

2. Taste and season the dip with a little more salt and black pepper, if needed. If you like it a bit creamier, add more coconut milk.

━● Tip … If you don't have a food processor, use a potato masher or a fork to mash the ingredients together.

SUN-DRIED TOMATO + CASHEW

Ingredients

1 cup (150g) unsalted raw cashews
½ cup (75g) sun-dried tomatoes
2 garlic cloves, peeled
¼ cup (40g) hemp seeds
a drizzle of extra virgin olive oil
a squeeze of lime juice
1 tbsp nutritional yeast (optional)
freshly ground black pepper

1. Add all the ingredients to a food processor with ½ cup (125ml) water and blend to the desired consistency, adding more water if needed. I blend the mixture for about 3 minutes to break down the cashews without making the dip too smooth (I like a little texture).

ROSEMARY CRACKERS

Makes 30

Crackers are usually relatively bland, so that whatever you pair them with will really stand out, but I love that my rosemary crackers are flavored with onion, garlic, and, of course, one of my favorite herbs, rosemary, so that they're tasty enough to be enjoyed on their own.

Ingredients

1 cup (100g) corn flour, plus extra for dusting
1½ cups (150g) rye flour, plus extra for dusting
½ tsp onion powder
¼ tsp garlic powder
1½ tsp dried rosemary
½ tsp pink Himalayan salt or sea salt
½ tsp freshly ground black pepper
½ tsp baking soda
¼ cup (60ml) olive oil

1. Preheat the oven to 325°F/170°C. Line two baking sheets with parchment paper.

2. Mix the flours together in a large bowl with the remaining dry ingredients.

3. Add the olive oil to the bowl and mix until the flour mixture is crumbly, then stir in ⅓ cup (100ml) water and mix to form a dough.

4. Roll out the dough on a floured surface until it is about ⅛ inch (3mm) thick. Cut the dough into 2–2½ inch (5cm) squares and use a fork to prick each cracker three times.

5. Place the crackers on the lined baking sheets and bake them for 30 minutes, turning the baking sheets halfway through the baking time, until they're crisp and golden.

6. Allow the crackers to cool and keep them in an airtight container.

OAT CAKES

Makes 18

If you aren't familiar with oat cakes, they're simply crackers that are made, predominantly, with oats. Their mild flavor pairs beautifully with a variety of sweet and savory dips and spreads, such as almond butter and hummus.

Ingredients

2¼ cups (225g) rolled oats
½ tsp baking soda
1 tsp dried oregano
2 tbsp extra-virgin olive oil
pink Himalayan salt or sea salt

1. Preheat the oven to 350°F/180°C. Line two baking sheets with parchment paper.

2. Pulse the oats in a food processor, but not too finely. A few whole oats are okay. Use ¼ cup (25g) of the oats to dust a work surface.

3. Mix together the oats, baking soda, a pinch of salt, and the oregano in a bowl, then stir in the olive oil and ½ cup (125ml) water to form a dough.

4. Roll out the dough on the oat-dusted surface until it's about ⅛ inch (3mm) thick.

5. Use a large cookie cutter or small water glass to cut the dough into 2½ inch (6cm) circles.

6. Place the oat cakes on the prepared baking sheets and bake them for 25 minutes, turning the baking sheets midway through the baking time, until they are crisp and golden.

7. Allow the oat cakes to cool and keep them in an airtight container.

ENERGY BALLS—3 WAYS

One of my favorite things to satisfy my hunger, and give me a boost, is energy balls. These fantastic snacks provide a healthy balance of fats, proteins, and carbs, as well as plenty of nutrients—exactly what you need to get through a long day. Keep energy balls in the fridge and bring a couple of them to work each day.

SUPERFOOD

Makes 10

Ingredients

2 tbsp quinoa
½ cup (80g) unsalted raw almonds
½ cup (60g) raisins
½ cup (90g) Medjool dates, pitted
¼ cup (30g) goji berries
1 tbsp chia seeds
1 tbsp maca powder

1. Place a saucepan over medium-high heat. Add the quinoa, cover the pan, and heat for 2–3 minutes, shaking the pan every few seconds. The quinoa will pop and slightly puff up.

2. Blend the almonds, raisins, dates, and goji berries in a food processor, until the mixture comes together. Add the remaining ingredients, including the quinoa, and roll the mixture into bite-size balls.

LEMON COCONUT BLISS

Makes 10

Ingredients

2 tbsp coconut oil
1 cup (90g) dried unsweetened coconut
1 tbsp lemon zest
½ cup (80g) unsalted raw Brazil nuts
1 tsp vanilla powder or 1 teaspoon organic vanilla extract
2 tbsp maple syrup
3 tbsp lemon juice

1. Set aside the coconut oil, 3-4 tablespoons of the coconut, and the lemon zest. Blend the remaining ingredients in a food processor until they're combined. Add the oil and pulse until combined.

2. Roll the mixture into bite-size balls and chill for 20 minutes.

3. Sprinkle the 3–4 tablespoons of coconut and the lemon zest onto a plate and roll the balls in the mix until they're fully covered.

SUPERGREEN

Makes 10

Ingredients

1 cup (180g) Medjool dates, pitted
¾ cup (115g) unsalted raw cashews
2 tsp spirulina
1 tsp wheatgrass
1 tbsp lime zest
1 tsp matcha powder

1. Blend all the ingredients, except the matcha, in a food processor, until the mixture comes together.

2. Roll the mixture into bite-size balls and chill for 20 minutes.

3. Sprinkle the matcha powder onto a plate. Roll the balls in the matcha powder to coat them.

RAW FIG + BAOBAB BARS

Makes 12

As much as I love healthy nut and fruit bars from health food stores, there's just nothing quite like making your own. I love the pop of the fig seeds and the sweetness from the golden raisins in these bars.

Ingredients

2 cups (320g)
    unsulphured
    dried figs (such as
    dried black mission
    figs)
2 cups (310g) unsalted
    raw cashews
½ cup (60g) golden
    raisins
¼ cup (30g)
    sunflower seeds
¼ cup (40g) flaxseed
2 tbsp baobab powder

1. Place the figs in a bowl, cover them with water, and then set them aside to soak for 1 hour.

2. Drain the figs and place all the ingredients, except for the baobab powder, in a food processor or blender, and pulse. Add the baobab powder and blend until the mixture is totally combined.

3. Bring the mixture together, then roll it out into a large rectangle until it's about ¼ inch (1cm) thick. It will be quite sticky.

4. Place the mixture in the freezer for 30 minutes to firm up, then neatly slice it into 1 x 4-inch (3.5 x 10-cm) bars, and keep them in an airtight container in the fridge.

CHOCOLATE-COATED BANANA POPSICLES

Makes 6–8

This is a really quick, easy, and delicious summer snack. The concept is simple, but full of flavor. The popsicle sticks can be bought from most craft stores. The chocolate dip is homemade and needs only three ingredients.

Ingredients

2 large ripe bananas, peeled and cut into ¼-inch (1cm) slices
2 tbsp almond butter
2 tbsp coconut oil
2 tbsp raw cacao powder
2 tbsp maple syrup
2 tbsp unsalted raw almonds

1. Spread each banana slice with almond butter and layer 3–4 slices on each stick.

2. Place the banana skewers on a plate and repeat the process with the remaining banana slices. Freeze them for an hour.

3. To make the chocolate dip, heat the coconut oil in a small saucepan over medium heat and remove the pan from the heat before it's completely melted. Whisk in the cacao powder and maple syrup. Pour the mixture into a bowl and put it to the side.

4. Crush the almonds in a mortar and pestle.

5. When the banana popsicles have been in the freezer for at least an hour, dip them in the chocolate until they're completely covered. Immediately sprinkle the crushed almonds over the chocolate and put the popsicles back in the freezer to set for about 30 minutes.

➤ Tip ... If you don't have time to make the chocolate dip from scratch, melt some dark chocolate instead.

CHOCOLATE + FIG POPCORN BARS

Makes 10

For most people, watching a film at home just isn't the same without a bowl of popcorn, but afterward you may crave something sweet. These sweet and salty bars fit the bill.

Ingredients

6 dried figs (try to buy 100% natural figs without sulphur dioxide)

½ tsp coconut oil, plus extra for greasing the pan

½ cup (60g) popcorn kernels

1 cup (150g) cacao butter

2½ tbsp raw cacao powder

3 tbsp pure maple syrup

¼ cup (60ml) almond butter

½ cup (75g) unsalted raw pistachios, chopped

pink Himalayan salt or sea salt

1. Place the figs in a bowl, then cover them with water and let them soak for at least 1 hour to soften.

2. Grease an 8-inch (20-cm) square baking pan and line it with parchment paper.

3. Heat the coconut oil in a large saucepan over medium heat. Add the popcorn and sprinkle over a pinch of salt. Give the saucepan a good shake and put the lid on.

4. It'll take a minute or so for the corn to start popping, and 5–7 minutes for all the kernels to pop. Keep shaking the pan to make sure the kernels are cooking evenly, and to keep the pan from burning.

5. To make the chocolate, melt the cacao butter in a small saucepan over low heat. Add the cacao powder and maple syrup to the pan and stir to combine.

6. Drain the figs and use the back of a fork to mash them into a paste. Stir the paste into the saucepan with the almond butter and half of the chopped pistachios, and remove the pan from the heat.

7. Transfer the popcorn to a large mixing bowl, discarding any kernels that haven't popped. Slowly pour the dark chocolate and fig mixture onto the popcorn, stirring as you go, to make sure the popcorn is fully covered.

8. Pour the mixture into the lined baking pan and use the back of a spoon to spread it out evenly, scattering the remaining pistachios over the top. Gently compress the mixture with the spoon and place it in the fridge for at least 2 hours to set, then slice it into 10 bars.

BLUEBERRY BURST DATES

Makes 10

I first tried cooked dates in Greece, and was surprised by how much they tasted like toffee. They were served as part of a savory mezze and sprinkled with sea salt. Here, I've added a rich ginger flavor to the mix. The blueberries burst when you bite into them, adding a sweet juicy taste.

Ingredients

10 Medjool dates
10 blueberries
3 tbsp tahini
1½ tsp ground ginger
pink Himalayan salt
   or sea salt

1. Preheat the oven to 325°F/170°C. Line a baking sheet with parchment paper.

2. Slice the dates down the middle, remove the pits, and spread them open. Sprinkle over a small amount of salt and place a blueberry in the middle of each date.

3. Place the dates on the baking sheet and bake for 15 minutes, checking them about halfway through. Remove the dates from the oven and let them cool down slightly.

4. Make the savory sauce by mixing the tahini with the ginger, and spoon about 1 teaspoon into each date.

Tip ... If you don't have tahini, try almond butter instead.

BOMBAY POPCORN

Serves 4

Popcorn is a wonderful snack alternative to chips, without all the additives and fat. Although popcorn is light, it keeps you feeling full, and you can experiment with different flavors. One of my favorite combinations is this Indian-inspired spice mix. Try it the next time you stay in to watch a movie.

Ingredients

1 tsp coconut oil
½ cup (110g)
    popcorn kernels
¼ tsp each of ground
    cumin, coriander,
    turmeric, and
    ground ginger, or
    1 tsp curry powder
pink Himalayan salt
    or sea salt and
    freshly ground
    black pepper

1. Heat the coconut oil in a large lidded saucepan over medium-high heat.

2. Once melted, add the popcorn kernels with the spices and a pinch of salt and pepper, then shake the pan to make sure all the kernels are coated.

3. Put the lid back on, turn the heat down to medium, and wait for the kernels to start to pop, shaking the pan occasionally.

4. When the popcorn has finished popping, remove the pan from the heat, and pour it into a large bowl, discarding any unpopped kernels.

Dessert

05

AFTER-DINNER TRUFFLES

Makes 10

A few years ago if you'd told me I could eat healthier truffles, I would have laughed, but then I discovered dates! Dates are deliciously sweet, and when combined with molasses, they provide a rich truffle flavor. These are a perfect evening treat when I'm watching my favorite TV program.

Ingredients

1 cup (200g) Medjool
   dates, pitted
½ cup (125g) unsalted
   peanut butter
½ cup (50g) rolled oats
1 tsp blackstrap
   molasses
a pinch of Himalayan
   pink salt or sea salt
2 tbsp raw cacao
   powder, to coat

1. Blend all the ingredients, except for the cacao powder, in a food processor until the mixture sticks together.

2. Roll into 10 bite-size balls and place in the fridge for 20 minutes.

3. Sprinkle the cacao powder onto a plate and roll each ball on the plate twice to make sure it's fully coated. Keep refrigerated in an airtight container.

—● Tip ... For a milder flavor, almond butter works really well in this recipe instead of peanut butter.

RASPBERRY + LEMON RIPPLE CHEESECAKE

Serves 10

This is a beautiful dessert and one I love to make when I want to impress the family. The mixture brings together two of my favorite colors and flavors: pink raspberry and yellow lemon. To recreate a cookie crust, I use pistachios and almonds for their crunchy texture.

Ingredients

crust
1 cup (180g) Medjool dates, pitted
¼ cup (40g) unsalted raw pistachios
¾ cup (115g) unsalted raw almonds

filling
1 lemon
1 x 14-oz (400-g) can coconut milk, refrigerated
2 cups (310g) unsalted raw cashews, soaked overnight
¼ cup (60ml) coconut nectar, agave nectar, or honey
¼ cup (60ml) coconut oil
seeds of 1 vanilla bean or 1 tsp organic vanilla extract
1¼ cups (185g) raspberries

2 tbsp pistachios, chopped, to serve
2 tbsp edible rose petals (optional), to serve

1. Blend all the crust ingredients together in a food processor until combined. Pour the mixture into an 8-inch (20-cm) springform pan and press down firmly with the back of a wooden spoon. Place the crust in the freezer to chill while you make the filling.

2. Zest the lemon and set the zest aside. Squeeze the juice from the lemon into a food processor or blender. Scoop out the solid coconut cream that has risen to the top of the can of coconut milk (this should be around 5 ounces/150g) and add this to the blender with a couple tablespoons of the milk. Drain the cashews and add the nuts with the remaining filling ingredients, except the raspberries, to the food processor. Blend until smooth and creamy.

3. Set aside ¼ cup (60ml) of the mixture. Stir ¾ cup (90g) of the raspberries and half the lemon zest into the remaining cheesecake mixture. Remove the crust from the freezer and pour half the cheesecake mixture on top.

4. Blend the reserved ¼ cup (60ml) of the cheesecake mixture with the remaining raspberries until totally smooth. Add half of this raspberry mixture, a tablespoon at a time, to the top of the cheesecake, gently swirling with a chopstick or the end of a spoon to create a marbled effect.

5. Pour over the remaining plain cheesecake mixture and smooth down. Again, add a tablespoon at a time of the remaining raspberry mixture and create a marbled effect. Gently shake the pan to smooth the top.

6. Mix the chopped pistachios with the rose petals, if using, and scatter on top of the cheesecake. Sprinkle the remaining lemon zest over the top and freeze for at least 4 hours, preferably overnight.

7. Thaw the cheesecake for 30 minutes before serving, or transfer to the fridge for about an hour and a half.

ORANGE + BASIL TART

Serves 10

I love to end a dinner party with this tart; it's sophisticated, light, and pleasing to the palate. The secret ingredient is steamed, pureed butternut squash, which makes a smooth and creamy filling. Don't be put off by vegetables in desserts. It's great to experiment with them, and when you get it right, it's so rewarding.

Ingredients

filling
½ butternut squash, peeled and chopped
1 x 14-oz (400-g) can of coconut milk, refrigerated
⅓ cup (75ml) maple syrup
1 tsp organic vanilla extract
zest of 1 orange, juice of ½
8–10 fresh basil leaves

crust
1½ cups (150g) ground almonds
¾ cup (135g) Medjool dates, pitted
1½ tbsp raw cacao powder
zest of 2 small oranges

topping
1 tbsp orange zest
a few fresh baby basil leaves

1. Place the squash in a lidded steamer basket. Steam for 15–20 minutes over a medium saucepan of simmering water until soft. Remove the pan from the heat and allow it to cool. (Run the squash under cold water to save time.)

2. Use a food processor to mix all the crust ingredients together until the mixture is sticky and holds together.

3. Press the crust mixture into a circular 8-inch (20-cm) fluted tart pan, making sure you press the crust right into the ridges, then keep the crust in the fridge while you make the filling.

4. Use a food processor or a hand whisk to puree the steamed butternut squash until smooth. You will only need 1 cup of this butternut squash puree, so if there's any leftover, save the rest for lunch!

5. Scoop out the solid coconut cream that has risen to the top of the can of coconut milk (this should be around 5 ounces/150g). Place the cream in the food processor with the remaining filling ingredients and blend until smooth.

6. Pour into the cooled crust and place in the fridge for a few hours to set, preferably overnight.

7. Serve the tart right after you take it out of the fridge. Garnish it with a grating of orange zest and a few baby basil leaves.

➤● Tip ... Refrigerating coconut milk in the can encourages the solids to separate from the liquid and rise to the top. These solids will give your tart a lovely creamy consistency.

APPLE + APRICOT CRUMBLE

Serves 4–6

My mum used to make a wonderful rhubarb crumble when I was younger; it is so nostalgic that I wanted to create my own version. I've paired apple with apricot—one of my favorite flavor combinations—and added oats, to make it more filling. Bring this crumble to the center of the table and let everyone dig in!

Ingredients

4 Granny Smith apples
4 tbsp coconut sugar
1 tsp ground cinnamon
a pinch of ground
    nutmeg
a pinch of
    ground cloves
½ tsp ground ginger
½ cup (90g)
    unsulphured dried
    apricots, quartered
1⅓ cups (200g)
    unsalted raw
    almonds
1¼ cups (125g)
    rolled oats
a pinch of pink
    Himalayan salt
    or sea salt
⅓ cup (75ml)
    coconut oil

1. Preheat the oven to 350°F/180°C.

2. Peel and core the apples and chop into rough ¾-inch (2-cm) chunks. Place in a medium saucepan over medium-low heat and add enough water to just cover the base of the pan. Cover the pan with a lid.

3. Simmer for 7 minutes over medium heat until softened and starting to break down, stirring occasionally, then remove from the heat.

4. Stir in 1 tablespoon of the sugar, the spices, and apricots, and set aside while you make the crumble.

5. In a small saucepan, make a caramel by heating the remaining coconut sugar with ¼ cup (60ml) water over medium heat. Keep stirring the sugar, and remove it from the heat when it has a thick, sticky consistency.

6. Finely chop ½ cup (50g) of the almonds in a food processor. Add the remaining almonds and ½ cup (50g) of the oats and blend until a crumbly mixture has formed. Put the mixture in a large bowl and combine with the remaining whole oats, caramel, and a pinch of salt.

7. Melt the coconut oil in a small saucepan over low heat, add to the bowl, and stir to combine.

8. Pour the stewed apple into an 8-inch (20-cm) square baking dish, add the crumble on top, and bake for 30 minutes.

🥣 Serving ideas ...
For a real treat, try this with my Pecan Ice Cream (see page 186).

PECAN ICE CREAM WITH SALTED CARAMEL SAUCE

Serves 4

We all have those moments when we crave ice cream, and you'd never guess this is made from plant-based ingredients. One of my favorite flavors is salted caramel pecan, and when dates are blended with salt, you get that same rich caramel flavor, without the refined sugar.

Ingredients

pecan ice cream
seeds of 1 vanilla bean
    or 1 tsp vanilla
    powder
½ cup (50g) unsalted
    raw pecan nuts
5 Medjool dates,
    pitted
1 cup (250ml)
    unsweetened
    almond milk
1 x 14-oz (400-g) can
    coconut milk
1 tbsp almond butter
a pinch of pink
    Himalayan salt or
    sea salt

salted caramel sauce
5 Medjool dates,
    pitted and soaked
½ cup (125ml)
    unsweetened
    almond milk
a pinch of pink
    Himalayan salt
    or sea salt

a handful of unsalted
    raw pecan nuts,
    chopped, to serve

1. To make the pecan ice cream, start by removing the seeds from the vanilla bean. Slice one side of the pod and gently open it. Use the knife or a teaspoon to scrape out the seeds.

2. Take half of the seeds or half of the vanilla powder, if using, and combine with half the pecans and the remaining ice cream ingredients in a blender for a few minutes until smooth.

3. Pour the mixture into a large plastic container, crumble in the remaining pecans, and stir.

4. Freeze for 3 hours, stirring every 30 minutes, if you can.

5. Make the salted caramel sauce. Drain the dates. With a blender, combine the dates with the almond milk and the remaining vanilla pod seeds or powder until totally smooth. Stir in the salt and keep in the fridge until you need it later.

6. After 3 hours of freezing, remove the ice cream from the freezer and use an electric mixer to whip the mixture so that it's extra smooth and creamy. You can place the ice cream back in the freezer for another hour. This is optional, so don't worry if you skip this step.

7. After the ice cream has been freezing for 4 hours, gently swirl in two thirds of the caramel sauce to make a ripple effect and place it back in the freezer overnight (or for at least another 2 hours).

8. Take the ice cream out of the freezer about 10–15
    minutes before serving to thaw slightly. Serve it with
    the remaining salted caramel sauce and sprinkle the
    crushed pecans on top.

    Tip ... Use this with my Pecan + Date Cookies (see page
    201) to make an ice cream sandwich.

BANANA MOCHA ICE CREAM CUPS

Makes 8

I don't have coffee too often, but once in a while, it's a wonderful hit of energy and a great addition to a dessert. These ice cream cups have only a subtle hint of coffee.

Ingredients

1 tbsp instant coffee
3 ripe bananas,
    peeled, sliced,
    and frozen
1 tsp organic vanilla
    extract
3 tbsp raw cacao
    powder
½ cup (125ml) canned
    coconut milk
2–3 tbsp maple syrup
dark chocolate,
    to serve
coffee beans,
    to serve

1. Dissolve the instant coffee with 1 tablespoon of boiling water and set it aside to cool slightly.

2. Place the frozen bananas in a food processor. Pulse until they are broken down, then blend at high speed until thickened and creamy.

3. Add the coffee, vanilla extract, cacao powder, coconut milk, and maple syrup to the food processor, and pulse again until combined, stopping every now and again to scrape the sides to make sure everything is combined.

4. Spoon the mixture into silicone cupcake liners and place them in the freezer for about 2 hours.

5. Remove the ice cream cups from the freezer 15 minutes before serving to soften. Grate dark chocolate over the top and place a coffee bean on each cup.

➤ Tip ... This recipe serves 8, so it's the perfect make-ahead dessert for a large dinner party.

CHOCOLATE COOKIE DOUGH ICE CREAM

Serves 4

One of the best things about frozen and blended bananas is that you get the consistency and creaminess of ice cream. This recipe is inspired by one of my old favorites while I was in college; cookie dough ice cream. Instead of a vanilla-flavored ice cream base, I made a chocolate one by adding cacao powder. This recipe is great for a night at home with friends and a good movie.

Ingredients

chocolate ice cream
6 frozen ripe
    bananas, peeled
1½ tsp organic
    vanilla extract
2 tbsp raw cacao
    powder
2 tbsp maple syrup
    (optional)

cookie dough pieces
¼ cup (25g) rolled oats
½ tbsp coconut oil
1 tbsp maple syrup
½ tbsp almond butter
¼ cup (25g) ground
    almonds
1 tbsp dark
    chocolate chips

a handful of
    raspberries,
    to serve

1. Grind the oats to a flour in a food processor.

2. Gently heat the coconut oil in a saucepan over low heat until melted. Remove from the heat, add the maple syrup and almond butter, and stir to combine.

3. In a large bowl, combine the ground almonds and oat flour. Stir in the coconut oil mixture to form the cookie dough. Allow it to cool slightly before adding the dark chocolate chips.

4. Roll the dough into small balls (use about ½ teaspoon of the mixture for each ball). Pinch the sides to make small cubes. Freeze them for about 10–15 minutes.

5. Meanwhile, make the ice cream. Blend the frozen bananas with the vanilla extract, cacao powder, and maple syrup, if using, in a blender until creamy and smooth.

6. Spoon the ice cream into two bowls and top with 5 cookie dough pieces each, along with some raspberries.

Tip ... If you have cookie dough left over, keep it in the fridge in an airtight container for an easy treat.

EASY WATERMELON SORBET

Serves 4

There is something about pairing watermelon with mint that is so refreshing. Watermelon is great for hydration and mint is really soothing, making the perfect combination. I love this, after a meal, or as a snack on a hot day.

Ingredients

½ watermelon
1 ripe banana, peeled
1 cup (250ml) fresh
    orange juice
    or water
a handful of fresh
    mint leaves
4 lemon wedges

1. Cut the watermelon into 1-inch (2-cm) thick chunks and remove any seeds. Freeze it for 5 hours or overnight, laying the chunks flat on a tray or plate so they don't stick together.

2. Once frozen, place the banana and juice or water in a blender. Blend until almost smooth. Add the mint leaves and continue blending until totally smooth.

3. Scoop into bowls and serve with a wedge of lemon to squeeze over the top.

 Tip ... These ingredients also make a nice smoothie; just blend them together instead of freezing.

ICE POPS—3 WAYS

I love making ice pops in the summer; they are super refreshing and a tasty way to cool down. These are made from 100% fruit and an easy dessert for a BBQ or picnic. When I know my younger cousins are coming, I always make a big batch—they particularly love the mango.

MANGO + COCONUT

Makes 2

Ingredients

1 lime
½ mango, peeled and pitted
1 tbsp dried unsweetened coconut

1. Zest the lime and set the zest aside.

2. Roughly chop the mango and place the pieces in a blender with the lime juice and ⅓ cup (80ml) water. Blend until smooth, then stir in the coconut and lime zest.

3. Pour into two popsicle molds and freeze for at least 5 hours, until solid.

APPLE COOLER

Makes 2

Ingredients

¼ cucumber, peeled
3 fresh mint leaves
1 green apple, peeled

1. Finely chop the cucumber and mint leaves. Roughly chop the remaining cucumber. Core and roughly chop the apple.

2. Place the apple and cucumber chunks into a blender with ¼ cup (60ml) water. Blend until smooth, then stir in the finely chopped mint and cucumber.

3. Pour into two popsicle molds and freeze for at least 5 hours, until solid.

SUMMER BERRY

Makes 2

Ingredients

¼ cup (30g) raspberries,
    plus 3 extra
¼ cup (40g) blueberries,
    plus 3 extra

1. Place the berries in a blender with ⅓ cup (80ml) water and blend until smooth.

2. Drop the extra berries into two popsicle molds, pour in the blended mixture, and freeze for at least 5 hours, until solid.

BALINESE BLACK RICE
PUDDING WITH MANGO

Serves 2

In Bali, a traditional breakfast dish is a black rice pudding, usually cooked by the grandmothers early in the morning. When I tried this for the first time, I fell in love. I wanted to make it into a dessert, because it's a bit too sweet for me for breakfast, but I love the simple flavor combination.

Ingredients

½ cup (100g)
    black rice
1 vanilla bean
4 tbsp canned
    coconut milk
2 tbsp coconut nectar
    or palm sugar
a pinch of pink
    Himalayan salt
    or sea salt

toppings
2 tbsp coconut flakes
½ mango, peeled,
    pitted, and diced
2 tbsp canned
    coconut milk
coconut nectar
    (optional)

1. Place the rice in a sieve and rinse thoroughly under cold running water. Soak the rice in a bowl of water for at least 1 hour, or overnight if possible. This will make the rice softer.

2. Drain the rice and add it to a saucepan with 1 cup (250ml) water. Bring to a boil with a pinch of salt, then turn the heat down to low, and simmer for 1 hour, adding more water, if the rice gets too dry, and stirring every now and again.

3. Once cooked, drain and return the rice to the pan. Slice the vanilla bean open, scrape out the seeds, and stir into the cooked rice with the coconut milk and the coconut nectar or sugar.

4. Toast the coconut flakes in a dry frying pan over medium-high heat for a couple of minutes until golden, stirring frequently, to prevent burning.

5. Garnish the rice with the mango, a drizzle of coconut milk, and a drizzle of coconut nectar, if you like. Scatter the toasted coconut on top and dig in.

Tip ... If you can't get hold of a vanilla bean use a teaspoon of vanilla extract.

CHOCOLATE + BANANA CHIA PUDDING

Serves 2

Pudding can seem mega indulgent, but when it's full of good stuff like avocado and banana, you're getting both flavor and nutrition. Adding the chia seeds brings a new dimension to the dish—they are hydrating and packed with nutrients for your brain and skin.

Ingredients

2 tbsp chia seeds
1 ripe banana, peeled
3 Medjool dates,
   pitted
½ ripe avocado,
   peeled and pitted
2 tbsp raw cacao
   powder
½ cup (125ml)
   unsweetened
   almond milk

1. Soak the chia seeds with 6 tablespoons of water in a bowl and refrigerate it for about 20 minutes.

2. Combine the remaining ingredients in a blender and blend until the mixture is smooth and the dates have broken up.

3. Stir in the soaked chia seeds and pour the mixture into two bowls or glasses. Add your choice of toppings and dig in.

❀ Topping ideas ...
A handful of fresh or frozen raspberries
Granola (see page 46)
A handful of pumpkin seeds
A dusting of cacao powder

BANANA + CHOC CHIP MUFFINS

Makes 8

I love straight-out-of-the-oven muffins. These are a nice treat to take with you on the go in-between meetings or to bake for the family. If you're working from home and craving an afternoon treat, they can be whipped up really quickly, with no need to cave in and snack on store-bought cookies!

Ingredients

dry ingredients
1½ cups (200g)
    spelt flour
1 tsp baking powder
3 tbsp coconut sugar
½ tsp vanilla powder
¼ cup (50g) dark
    chocolate chips
    (dairy-free)

wet ingredients
3 heaping tbsp
    coconut oil
3 ripe bananas,
    peeled
⅓ cup (80ml)
    unsweetened
    almond milk

1. Preheat the oven to 180°C/350°F. Line an 8-cup muffin pan with paper muffin liners.

2. In a large bowl, mix together all the dry ingredients apart from the chocolate chips.

3. Melt the coconut oil in a small saucepan over low heat. Mash the bananas with a fork and mix with the melted coconut oil and almond milk. Pour the mixture into the bowl of dry ingredients and stir in the chocolate chips.

4. Spoon the mixture evenly into the muffin pan and bake for 25–30 minutes until an inserted knife comes out clean. Allow the muffins to cool in the pan for 5 minutes, then transfer them to a wire rack to cool completely.

━━● Tip ... If your bananas aren't quite ripe, place them in a brown paper bag with an apple or pear for a few hours. I find this helps them ripen more quickly.

PECAN + DATE COOKIES

Makes 18

Rather than spending hours looking for presents at the mall or online, why not bring these to the next birthday party or event instead? I love to wrap these in pretty brown paper and some string. They look great and will keep for a few days after the party.

Ingredients

2 tbsp milled flaxseed
2 cups (200g) rolled oats
1 cup (125g) unsalted raw pecan nuts, finely chopped
½ tsp ground cinnamon
½ tsp baking soda
a pinch of pink Himalayan salt or sea salt
1 cup (180g) Medjool dates, preferably soaked overnight
½ tsp organic vanilla extract

1. Preheat the oven to 170°C/325°F. Line two baking sheets with parchment paper.

2. Mix the flaxseed with 3 tablespoons of water and set it aside to thicken for at least 10 minutes.

3. Grind half the oats into a flour in a food processor and mix with the whole oats, chopped pecan nuts, cinnamon, baking soda, and a pinch of salt.

4. Place the dates, 2 tablespoons of water (if you soaked your dates, use the soaking water here), and vanilla extract in a food processor and blend until smooth. Stir in the flaxseed mixture, which should have thickened by now.

5. In a large bowl, combine the dry ingredients and fold into the date mixture to form the cookie dough.

6. Scoop a heaping tablespoon of the dough onto the lined baking sheet. Use your fingers to press down to create a round shape.

7. Repeat until all the dough has been used. Bake for 10–12 minutes.

8. Allow the cookies to cool before removing them from the parchment paper and store in an airtight container.

➤ Tip ... Soaking the dates softens them, and using the soaking water in the recipe adds delicious flavor. Simply place the dates in a bowl of water overnight.

ORANGE SPICED COOKIES

Makes 18

This is a lovely festive treat. It has all the typical ingredients that you would find in Christmas pudding in the form of a light delicious cookie. There is something about the smell of oranges and cinnamon that reminds me so much of Christmas, and ground almonds give the cookies a nutty texture and taste.

Ingredients

dry ingredients
1½ cups (150g)
    ground almonds
1½ cups (200g)
    spelt flour
1 tsp baking soda
1 tsp ground cinnamon
½ tsp ground ginger
¼ tsp ground nutmeg
a pinch of ground
    cloves
½ cup (115g)
    coconut sugar

wet ingredients
½ cup (125ml)
    coconut oil
1 orange
1 tbsp black strap
    molasses
1 tsp apple cider
    vinegar

1. Preheat the oven to 375°F/ 190°C. Line two baking sheets with parchment paper.

2. Combine the dry ingredients, except the coconut sugar, in a large bowl and set it aside.

3. Gently heat the coconut oil in a small saucepan over low heat until just melted. Remove from the heat and beat with the coconut sugar by hand or with an electric mixer until combined.

4. Zest the orange and set the zest aside. In a large bowl, squeeze in the juice from the orange and pour in the remaining wet ingredients the coconut sugar and melted coconut oil.

5. Use an electric mixer to mix on high speed for about 1 minute.

6. Gently fold in the dry ingredients with the orange zest, adding one half at a time, until combined.

7. Divide the mixture into 18 balls and place them on the baking sheets. Flatten them into 2-inch (5-cm) rounds and bake for 10–12 minutes until golden.

━● Tip ... To make this nut-free, swap the ground almonds for ground oats.

JAMMY SANDWICH COOKIES

Makes 25

I have so many school-day memories of opening my lunch box and finding one of these cookies inside. They're great to have in the cookie jar if someone stops by unexpectedly. No one will guess the ingredients are natural and wholesome.

Ingredients

½ cup (60ml)
   Strawberry Chia
   Jam (see page 56)

dry ingredients
1½ cups (150g)
   ground almonds
2 cups (260g)
   buckwheat flour
1 tsp baking powder
½ tsp ground ginger
½ tsp ground
   cinnamon
a pinch of pink
   Himalayan salt
   or sea salt

wet ingredients
½ cup (125ml) coconut
   oil, melted
½ cup (125ml)
   maple syrup
1 tsp organic
   vanilla extract
1 tsp vanilla powder

1. Preheat the oven to 325°F/170°C and line two large baking sheets with parchment paper.

2. In a large mixing bowl, mix the dry ingredients together.

3. Combine the wet ingredients and pour them into the bowl with the dry ingredients. Mix until a dough forms. If the mixture is a little too wet to work with, place it in the fridge to chill and firm up.

4. Flour a clean surface and roll the dough out until it is ¼-inch (5mm) thick. Use a 2-inch (4-cm) circular cookie cutter or a glass to cut 50 circles out of the dough, re-rolling as needed.

5. Use a small heart-shaped cookie cutter to cut out small hearts in the center of 25 of the pastry circles, then carefully place all of them on the lined baking sheets. (Use a spatula or palette knife to do this to prevent them from breaking).

6. Bake for 10–12 minutes or until lightly golden. Allow it to cool before adding ½ teaspoon of jam to the center of each plain cookie and then topping it with one of the cookies that has a heart cut out.

━● Tip ... If you don't have a heart-shaped cookie cutter, you can use a knife to cut out little heart shapes.

Makes 10

I travel to the US a lot, and I always see cinnamon rolls in cafés and bakeries—and I'm not surprised! I wanted to create a plant-based version of these rolls, so I could serve them for the holiday season. To avoid the usual large amounts of butter, I've used coconut oil.

Ingredients

dough
2 tbsp milled flaxseed
1 cup (250ml) unsweetened almond milk
1⅞ cups (285g) whole-wheat flour
1⅓ cups (150g) spelt flour
3 tbsp coconut sugar
2 tsp quick-action yeast or 1 x ¼-oz (7g) packet
½ tsp organic vanilla extract
1 tbsp olive oil

filling
⅛ cup (30ml) coconut oil
⅙ cup (40ml) maple syrup
1 tbsp ground cinnamon
¼ cup (30g) golden raisins
½ cup (50g) chopped unsalted raw pecan nuts

1. Mix the flaxseed with 3 tablespoons of water and set aside to thicken. Meanwhile, heat the almond milk in a saucepan over low heat until slightly warmed but not hot.

2. Mix together the flours, sugar, and yeast in a large bowl. Stir the vanilla extract into the warm milk and create a well in the middle of the dry ingredients. Pour the almond milk into the well and stir in the flaxseed mixture and the oil. Combine all the ingredients to form the dough.

3. Knead the dough on a lightly floured surface for 5 minutes. If the dough feels too wet, add an extra tablespoon of spelt flour.

4. Cover the bowl with plastic wrap and keep it in a warm place for 1–2 hours or until it has doubled in size.

5. For the filling, melt the coconut oil in a small saucepan over low heat. Add the maple syrup, cinnamon, golden raisins, and pecans and remove the pan from the heat.

6. Flour a clean surface and roll out the dough into a large rectangular shape, about 18 by 12 inches (45cm x 30cm).

7. Spread the filling onto the dough evenly, leaving about ¾ inch (2cm) free around the edges.

8. Roll the dough from one long edge to form a log shape. Seal the end of the log by dipping your finger in water, wetting the edge of the rectangle, and gently pressing it into the rolled dough.

(recipe continues on the next page)

maple glaze
¼ cup (25g) unsalted
    raw pecan nuts
2 tbsp maple syrup
¼ cup (60ml)
    unsweetened
    almond milk
1 tbsp coconut oil
a pinch of pink
    Himalayan salt
    or sea salt

1. Use a sharp knife to slice off and discard about ¾ inch (2cm) from each end. Slice the rest of the log into 1½-inch (4-cm) round slices (you should get ten).

2. Place each roll face up in a medium 8-inch (20-cm) round baking pan, lightly greased with coconut oil, packed in tightly. Leave for 30 more minutes or until slightly puffed up.

3. Preheat the oven to 350°F/180°C.

4. Bake the rolls for 30 minutes, until nicely browned. Remove them from the oven and allow them to cool while you make the maple glaze.

5. Blend together all the glaze ingredients until totally smooth. Keep the glaze in the fridge for a few minutes to set, then drizzle it generously over the rolls.

➤ Tip ... I use flaxseed mixed with water to replace eggs in baked goods. Or I sometimes simply add a tablespoon to my smoothies in the morning for the added health kick.

ONE-DISH BAKED COOKIES

Serves 4

Growing up I used to love premade cookie dough as a treat. We would bring it home, squeeze all the dough onto a baking sheet and pop it in the oven. This is my take on a guilty pleasure—cookies that are full of delicious ingredients, and which can be eaten right out of the oven.

Ingredients

¼ cup (60ml) coconut oil, plus extra, for greasing
1 cup (100g) rolled oats
1 cup (100g) ground almonds
¼ cup (50g) coconut sugar or brown sugar
1 tsp baking powder
¼ cup (60ml) unsweetened apple sauce
¼ cup (60ml) unsweetened almond milk
1 tsp organic vanilla extract
½ cup (100g) dark chocolate chips (dairy-free)
a pinch of pink Himalayan salt

1. Preheat the oven to 350°F/180°C. Grease an 8-inch (20-cm) square baking pan with some coconut oil and line with parchment paper.

2. Grind the oats in a food processor into a fine flour and transfer to a large bowl. Mix in the ground almonds, sugar, and baking powder with a pinch of salt.

3. Melt the coconut oil in a medium saucepan over low heat and pour it into the bowl of dry ingredients, along with the apple sauce, almond milk, and vanilla extract. Stir to combine.

4. Add the chocolate chips. Pour the mixture into the lined baking pan and smooth the top. Bake for 15–20 minutes or until golden. Divide into 4 square cookies or if you can't wait, like me, eat them straight out of the pan!

BLACK BEAN BANANA BROWNIES

Makes 8

When I first made these brownies, I asked my friends to guess what the secret ingredient was—they had no idea it was black beans. I love that these brownies are as rich as traditional ones, but are higher in protein and more filling. They are perfect for a post-gym treat.

Ingredients

coconut oil,
  for greasing
2 ripe bananas, peeled
1 x 14-oz (400-g) can
  black beans,
  drained
¼ cup (30g) raw
  cacao powder
¼ cup (30g) brown
  rice flour
¼ cup (60g)
  almond butter
½ cup (125ml)
  agave nectar or
  maple syrup
½ cup (60ml)
  unsweetened
  almond milk
½ tsp baking powder
1 tsp organic vanilla
  extract
¼ cup (25g) unsalted
  raw walnuts, plus
  5 for topping

1. Preheat the oven to 350°F/180°C. Grease an 8-inch (20-cm) square cake pan with coconut oil and line with parchment paper.

2. Add all the ingredients, except for the walnuts, to a food processor. Blend until smooth.

3. Add the walnuts to the mixture and blend for a couple of seconds until the walnuts have broken down into chunks (or use store-bought chopped walnuts and stir them in).

4. Pour the mixture into the pan. Crush the remaining 5 walnuts and sprinkle them over the brownie mixture. Bake for 20 minutes. Allow the brownies to cool fully in the pan before slicing into 8 squares.

CHOCOLATE CUPCAKES WITH COCONUT CREAM FROSTING

Makes 12

I love cupcakes, but then again who doesn't? I didn't think it would be possible to make a plant-based version that tasted so good, but after many sessions in the kitchen, I finally found a mixture that worked. The rich coconut cream frosting is so delicious. It's very tempting to eat it straight from the bowl.

Ingredients

1½ cups (260g) brown rice flour
½ cup (60g) raw cacao powder
½ tsp baking soda
1 tsp baking powder
1 cup (250g) plain coconut yogurt
½ cup (100g) coconut sugar
¾ cup (180ml) unsweetened almond milk
1 tsp organic vanilla extract
1 tsp apple cider vinegar

coconut cream frosting
½ x 14-oz (400-g) can coconut milk, refrigerated
2 tbsp raw cacao powder, plus extra for dusting
2 tbsp maple syrup
½ tsp organic vanilla extract
½ tsp arrowroot powder
2 tbsp raw cacao nibs, to decorate

1. Preheat the oven to 350°F/180°C and line one or two muffin pans with 12 paper cupcake liners.

2. Start by mixing the rice flour, cacao powder, baking soda, and baking powder together in a bowl and set aside.

3. In a separate large bowl, use an electric mixer to whip the coconut yogurt together with the coconut sugar. Gradually add the almond milk, whisking as you pour. Fold in the vanilla extract and apple cider vinegar.

4. Gradually fold the dry ingredients into the wet ingredients, until they are just combined. Avoid overmixing the batter.

5. Divide the mixture between the cupcake liners and bake for 25 minutes, or until cooked through. To check whether the cakes are cooked, insert a knife into the center of one cake—if the knife comes out clean they are done; if still sticky, return to the oven and bake for 5 more minutes or until an inserted knife comes out clean. Remove from the oven and allow the cakes to cool on a wire rack.

(recipe continues on the next page)

6. While the cupcakes are cooling, make the coconut cream frosting. Scoop out the solid coconut cream that has risen to the top of the can of coconut milk (this should be around 5 ounces/150g) and place in a large bowl. Use an electric mixer to whisk all the frosting ingredients together until thickened and the bowl can be turned upside down without the mixture moving. If it's not thick enough, keep it in the fridge for about 20 minutes before spreading on the cupcakes.

7. Once the cupcakes have totally cooled (this is important), smoothly spread the coconut cream frosting onto each cake. Finish with a dusting of cacao powder and a sprinkling of cacao nibs over the cakes. Keep the frosted cupcakes refrigerated in an airtight container.

DATE, WALNUT + BANANA LOAF

Serves 10

One of my favorite things to do with friends is share afternoon tea; it's a great way to see old friends and gossip over cake. This loaf is perfect for slicing up and sharing. There's something very wholesome about the combination of bananas and dates, with the added crunch from the walnuts.

Ingredients

coconut oil,
    for greasing
2½ ripe bananas,
    peeled
1½ cups (200g)
    buckwheat flour
¼ cup (25g)
    chopped unsalted
    raw walnuts
1 tsp baking powder
1 tsp baking soda
⅔ cup (110g) Deglet
    Nour Dates, pitted
    and chopped
¾ cup (190ml)
    unsweetened
    almond milk
a pinch of Himalayan
    pink salt or sea salt

1. Preheat the oven to 325°F/170°C and grease an 8 x 4-inch (20 x 10-cm) loaf pan with a little coconut oil and line with parchment paper.

2. Mash 2 bananas and slice the remaining half-banana.

3. In a large bowl, combine the flour, walnuts, baking powder, baking soda, and a pinch of salt.

4. Stir in the mashed and sliced bananas and chopped dates and slowly add the almond milk until the mixture is fully combined.

5. Pour the mixture into the pan and bake for 35–40 minutes or until golden and cooked through. To check whether the loaf is cooked, insert a knife into the center—if it comes out clean it is done; if still sticky, return the loaf to the oven and bake for 15 more minutes or until an inserted knife comes out clean.

6. Allow the loaf to cool in the pan for 10 minutes before turning out onto a wire rack to cool completely.

🥣 Serving ideas ...
Try spreading a slice with almond butter or one of my homemade chia jams (see page 56).

CARROT CAKE LOAF + LEMON "CREAM CHEESE"

Serves 10

Baking has always been part of my life. It has a wonderful way of getting the whole family into the kitchen, and carrot cake is one of my favorites. Just remember, cake doesn't have to be bad for you. It's all about what you throw into the mixing bowl!

Ingredients

½ cup (120ml) melted coconut oil, plus extra for greasing
1 cup (130g) spelt flour
1 cup (115g) almond flour
¾ cup (90g) unsalted raw walnuts, chopped
½ cup (60g) raisins
1 tsp ground cinnamon
½ tsp ground nutmeg
½ tsp ground ginger
2 tsp baking powder
1 tsp baking soda
2 small carrots, peeled and finely grated (you need 4 oz/115g)
½ cup (120ml) unsweetened almond milk
½ cup (120ml) maple syrup
2 teaspoons organic vanilla extract
1 tsp apple cider vinegar

topping
½ cup (80g) unsalted raw cashews, soaked
1 tbsp coconut nectar or maple syrup
½ tsp vanilla powder
3-5 tbsp unsweetened almond milk
½ lemon

1. Preheat the oven to 350°F/180°C. Grease a 8 x 4-inch (20 x 10-cm) loaf pan with coconut oil and line with parchment paper.

2. In a large mixing bowl, combine the flours, ⅔ cup (80g) walnuts, raisins, spices, baking powder, baking soda, and 3 ounces (100g) grated carrot. Toss well to combine thoroughly. This is key, or all your fruit and nuts will sink to the bottom of the loaf! In another bowl, combine the almond milk, coconut oil, maple syrup, vanilla, and vinegar. This helps the loaf rise.

3. Add the wet ingredients to the dry and mix until fully combined. Spoon into the lined pan and bake for 60–70 minutes, until cooked through and nicely browned on top. (Don't be tempted to open the oven door before the baking time is done.) Remove the pan from the oven. Let the cake cool in the pan for 20 minutes, then place it on a cooling rack and let it cool completely.

4. To make the topping, drain the cashews and place them in a food processor. Pulse until the nuts are broken up. Add the coconut nectar, vanilla powder, and almond milk. Finely grate in the lemon zest and add a squeeze of juice. Blend for a few minutes until the mixture is smooth and creamy, adding more milk if necessary.

5. Transfer the topping into a bowl and refrigerate for 10 minutes, while the cake cools.

6. Spoon the topping onto the cooled cake and sprinkle the remaining chopped walnuts and grated carrots on top.

LITY:
THER
bonds between people in a group, such as a family. Eating and drinking together plays a large role in organizing a society today—such as who invites whom, who sits next to whom—and it played an equally large role in the past, when commensality was the practice for negotiating social relations and hierarchies. Hierarchy, heterarchy, closeness of relations and power relations are all expressed in commensality—and that applies to family dinners as much as formal dinners for foreign heads of state.
WHY IS IT IMPORTANT THAT FAMILIES COME TOGETHER FOR MEALS? WHAT ISSUES COME FROM EATING ALONE?
Morten: If we eat on our own when we feel like it—which I'm sure we're actually more comfortable doing—we're expressing a strong distrust of society. If family members don't regularly eat together, they're basically declaring the family to be a common name and address, nothing more. It should be noted that for commensality to exist, there must be equal access to all foods. The reason we have societies is so that we can be better together than any individual member can be alone. So having a simple inclusive discussion of everything, which can be part of eating together, will improve everyone's ability to make points and understand them.
IN WHAT WAYS DOES COMMENSALITY IMPACT OUR EMOTIONAL AND PHYSICAL HEALTH?
Morten: Because eating is a time of vulnerability, we're often more comfortable eating on our own. But it's unhealthy for us to do so—emotionally as well as physically, because we constantly need to practice our social skills and experience the enjoyment of being with other people and performing "togetherness." Some people have so much trouble doing this that it could be regarded as an emotional disorder.
WHAT DOES THE TERM FAMILY MEAN TO YOU?
Morten: I don't like the idea of "blood relatives" as a concept. Families are based on unions of people who aren't specifically blood relatives.
Susanne: I agree that families being made up of blood relatives is a rather strange concept, as it excludes stepmothers, adopted children, a husband and wife alone, etc. We should ignore that and define family in the sense of a small group of people living together—for example, a group of youngsters living together while studying who form a kind of surrogate family. Inviting more people into this definition opens us up to a wider social commensality.

RED BEET CAKE WITH CHOCOLATE GANACHE

Serves 10

Don't knock this cake until you try it. Even if you don't like beets, you won't be able to taste them once they're mixed with chocolate—and the ganache means your friends won't guess it's plant-based. If you want to make a birthday cake for a friend, this will seriously impress.

Ingredients

wet ingredients
½ cup (125ml) coconut oil, plus extra for greasing
1½ cups (300g) apple sauce
2 cups (500ml) unsweetened almond milk
1 tsp apple cider vinegar

dry ingredients
1 cup (100g) rolled oats
2¼ cups (400g) brown rice flour
1½ cups (150g) coconut sugar
⅔ cup (80g) raw cacao powder
2 tsp baking powder
1 tsp baking soda
a pinch of pink Himalayan salt or sea salt
3 medium red beets, peeled and finely grated

chocolate ganache
4 oz (100g) dark chocolate, 70% cocoa solids (dairy-free)
1 cup (155g) unsalted raw cashews, soaked overnight
¾ cup (185ml) unsweetened almond milk

1. Preheat the oven to 350°F/180°C. Grease two 8-inch (20-cm) cake pans with coconut oil.

2. Melt the coconut oil in a small saucepan over low heat.

3. Grind the oats to a flour in a food processor, put it in a large bowl, and mix it with the rest of the dry ingredients, except the beets. In a separate bowl, combine the melted coconut oil with the remaining wet ingredients.

4. Make a well in the middle of the dry ingredients and fold in the wet mixture until fully combined. Stir in the grated beets, setting aside 2 tablespoons for later.

5. Divide the mixture evenly between the cake pans and bake for 30 minutes or until an inserted knife comes out clean. Carefully transfer to a cooling rack and allow to cool.

6. To make the chocolate ganache, break up the dark chocolate and place it in a heatproof bowl. Set the bowl above a saucepan of water simmering over low heat to melt the chocolate.

7. Drain the cashews and blend them with the almond milk until smooth. Pour this mixture into another bowl.

8. Stir the melted chocolate into the cashew and almond milk and place it in the fridge to firm up for 20 minutes.

9. Spread a third of the ganache onto one of the cooled cakes. Place the other cake on top and smooth the remaining ganache over the top and sides with a palette knife.

10. Decorate the cake with the reserved grated beets, and a dusting of cacao, or a grating of chocolate, if you like.

OAT BARS—3 WAYS

Commercial oat bars are delicious, but they're usually made with sugar or artificial sweeteners. I love the taste, though, so I had to make my own healthy version. I make a batch if I'm having my girlfriends over, and they are also great as a grab-and-go breakfast.

BLUEBERRY + COCONUT

Makes 12

Ingredients

3 ripe bananas, peeled
3 cups (300g) rolled oats
1 cup (90g) dried unsweetened coconut
1 cup (150g) blueberries
⅓ cup (90ml) coconut oil,
    plus extra for greasing
¼ cup (50g) coconut sugar

1. Preheat the oven to 350°F/180°C. Lightly grease a deep 8-inch (20-cm) square baking pan with coconut oil and line with parchment paper.

2. Mash the bananas with the back of a fork until smooth and set aside.

3. Mix together the oats and coconut in a large bowl and stir in the blueberries.

4. Melt the coconut oil in a small saucepan over low heat. Add the coconut sugar and stir for a couple of minutes to dissolve, then stir in the mashed bananas.

5. Add the coconut and banana mixture to the bowl of dry ingredients and stir to completely combine.

6. Pour the mixture into the pan, smooth the top with the back of a wooden spoon, and bake for 30 minutes, until golden.

7. While the cake is still warm, slice it into 12 squares and allow them to cool in the pan. Once cooled, keep the oat bars in an airtight container. Perfect for a grab-and-go snack!

BANANA, GOLDEN RAISIN + THYME

Makes 12

Ingredients

⅓ cup (90ml) coconut oil,
    plus extra for greasing
3 ripe bananas, peeled
1 cup (150g) unsalted raw almonds
3 cups (300g) rolled oats
½ cup (60g) golden raisins
12 fresh thyme sprigs, leaves
    picked or 2 tsp dried thyme
3 tbsp coconut sugar

1. Preheat the oven to 350°F/180°C.
   Lightly grease a deep 8-inch (20-cm)
   square baking pan with coconut oil
   and line with parchment paper.

2. Mash 2 of the bananas with the back
   of a fork and slice the other one.

3. Crush the almonds with a mortar and
   pestle into small chunks, then mix
   with the oats and golden raisins in a
   large bowl.

4. Roughly chop the thyme sprigs and
   stir about 2 tablespoons of the
   leaves into the oats.

5. Melt the coconut oil in a small
   saucepan over low heat. Remove the
   oil from the heat, stir in the mashed
   bananas and coconut sugar, then mix
   into the oats with the sliced banana.

6. Pour the mixture into the pan. Use
   the back of a wooden spoon to press
   the mixture down and bake for 25
   minutes until golden.

7. While still warm, slice into squares
   and allow to cool in the pan. Once
   cooled, keep in an airtight container.

PEANUT BUTTER + JAM

Makes 12

Ingredients

coconut oil, for greasing
2 ripe bananas, peeled
1 cup (250g) crunchy peanut butter
½ cup (125ml) unsweetened almond milk
¼ cup (40g) coconut sugar
3 cups (300g) rolled oats
1 cup (250ml) Strawberry Chia Jam
    (see page 56), or 100% fruit
    strawberry jam, refrigerated

1. Preheat the oven to 350°F/180°C.
   Lightly grease a medium 8-inch
   (20-cm) square baking pan with
   a little coconut oil and line with
   parchment paper.

2. Mash the bananas with a fork until
   smooth and place in a large mixing
   bowl. Stir in the peanut butter,
   almond milk, and coconut sugar until
   combined, then add the oats.

3. Pour a little more than half of
   the mixture into the pan. Use the
   back of a spoon to compress the
   mixture down evenly and bake for 15
   minutes.

4. Pour over the jam and smooth it down.
   Now add the remaining oat mixture
   by adding about a tablespoon at a
   time over the top. This layer will be
   rough, so don't worry about trying to
   smooth it down. You will be able to
   see patches of jam.

5. Bake for another 20–25 minutes until
   golden.

6. While the cake is still warm, cut it
   into 12 squares. Allow them to cool
   for about 10 minutes before removing
   them from the tray.

Drinks

06

HOMEMADE REFRESHING LEMONADE

Makes 4 cups

When my mum had a baby shower for my little sister, I wanted to provide a delicious non-alcoholic drink. As it was the height of summer, I decided on a refreshing homemade lemonade, sweetened with natural agave nectar or honey, to cool everyone down.

Ingredients

1-inch (2.5-cm) piece
    of fresh ginger,
    peeled and sliced
4 tbsp honey or
    agave nectar
¼ bunch of fresh mint,
    leaves picked
6 lemons

1. Bring 4 cups (1 liter) of water to a boil in a large saucepan, then turn the heat down to low.

2. Add the ginger, 5 mint leaves, and the juice from 5 of the lemons (about ¾ cup/200ml) to the water with the honey and sugar. Leave for 20 minutes on very low heat for the flavors to infuse.

3. Strain the lemonade into a pitcher and discard the ginger and mint. Chill the lemonade in the fridge for at least 1–2 hours or until cold.

4. Slice the remaining lemon and serve the chilled lemonade with ice cubes, lemon slices, and the remaining fresh mint leaves.

━● Tip … To get the most juice from the lemons, try rolling them on a hard surface before you slice them; this releases their juices.

MOCKTAILS—3 WAYS

These drinks are perfect for quenching your thirst and cooling you off on a hot summer's day, especially when served ice-cold. The Pina Coolada will transport you to a beach in Hawaii, the Virgin Mary to a cocktail bar in New York, and the Cucumber and Melon muddler is fit for a spa.

PINA COOLADA

Serves 1

Ingredients

1 tbsp canned coconut milk, refrigerated
½ cup (100g) fresh pineapple chunks
1 cup (250ml) coconut water
½ tsp organic vanilla essence or extract
juice of ½ lime

1. Scoop out 1 tablespoon of the solid coconut cream that has risen to the top of the can of coconut milk and place in a blender.

2. Add the remaining ingredients, combine in the blender, and serve in a glass over crushed ice.

CUCUMBER + MELON MUDDLER

Serves 1

Ingredients

½ cucumber, chopped
2 celery stalks
¼ honeydew melon, seeded, flesh
**   scooped out, and cut into chunks**
8 fresh mint leaves,
**   plus 1 sprig to serve**
juice of ½ lemon

1. Run the cucumber, celery, melon, and mint through a juicer and pour into a glass with 3 tablespoons water.

2. Squeeze the lemon juice into the glass, stir, and serve with the fresh mint sprig.

VIRGIN MARY

Serves 1

Ingredients

4 large vine-ripened tomatoes
2 celery stalks, trimmed
juice of ½ lemon
a small pinch of cayenne pepper
pink Himalayan salt or sea salt and
**   freshly ground black pepper**

1. Run the tomatoes and 1 celery stalk through a juicer.

2. Stir in the lemon juice and cayenne and serve in a glass with a small celery stalk and a pinch of salt and black pepper.

━━● Tip ... To make these into fun cocktails, add 1 ounce (25ml) of rum to the Pina Coolada, 1 ounce (25ml) of vodka to the Virgin Mary, and 1 ounce (25ml) of gin to the Cucumber + Melon Muddler.

MAPLE MATCHA LATTE

Serves 1

This is a real energy-booster, perfect for an early morning pick-me-up, and a great alternative to coffee.

Ingredients

1 cup (250ml) unsweetened almond milk
1 tsp matcha powder
1 tsp maple syrup, plus extra to sweeten
¼ tsp vanilla powder or ½ tsp organic vanilla extract

1. Heat the almond milk in a saucepan over medium heat until simmering.

2. Put the matcha powder into a mug and add ¼ cup (60ml) boiling water. Whisk to dissolve the powder and stir in the maple syrup and vanilla powder.

3. Pour the hot milk into a latte glass and stir in the matcha mixture. If using frothed milk, carefully pour the matcha mixture close to one side of the glass to keep the milk lovely and foamy. Add extra maple syrup to sweeten, if needed.

Tip ... If you have a milk frother, use it to make this recipe.

MORNING DETOX DRINK

Serves 1

I like to kick-start my days with a hot detox drink—the zingy lemon and hot cayenne pepper give a real wake-up call.

Ingredients

1 ¼-inch (1-cm) piece
  of fresh ginger,
  peeled and sliced
½ tsp ground
  cinnamon
a pinch of cayenne
  pepper
1 tsp honey or
  maple syrup
juice of ½ lemon

1. Add the ginger to a mug with the cinnamon, cayenne pepper, and honey. Squeeze in the lemon juice and mix.

2. Add boiling water, stir, and leave to brew for 5 minutes.

SLEEPY BREW

Serves 1

In the evenings, I want a milky drink that calms the body and mind, but is also made from incredible ingredients. My recipe uses maca to add a slight caramel flavor.

Ingredients

1 cup (250ml)
  unsweetened
  almond milk
2 teaspoons
  maca powder
1 tsp barley
  malt extract
½ tsp vanilla powder
  or 1 tsp organic
  vanilla extract

1. Heat the almond milk in a saucepan over medium heat.

2. Place the maca powder, barley malt extract, and vanilla powder in your favorite mug. Pour the milk on top and whisk until the maca powder is dissolved and serve.

JEWELED ICE CUBES

Makes 16 ice cubes (4 of each flavor)

I'm the kind of person who has to really remind herself to drink water throughout the day to stay hydrated. Adding these fruity ice cubes to a glass of water infuses it with a subtle flavor and looks so beautiful—far more appealing than just plain water.

Ingredients

lime + passion fruit
½ lime, cut into
    small chunks
1 passion fruit, pulp
    and seeds
    scooped out

raspberries + mint
4 raspberries
4 small fresh
    mint leaves

lemon + blueberry
½ lemon, cut into
    small chunks
4 blueberries

cucumber + lemon
1 ¾-inch (2cm) piece
    of cucumber, cut
    into small chunks
½ lemon, cut into
    small chunks

1. Lay out all the ingredients. Place the ingredients into the compartments of a large ice cube tray in their respective combinations to make four ice cubes of each variety.

2. Top each compartment with water and freeze overnight.

3. These go well with sparkling water or even with my Homemade Refreshing Lemonade (see page 225).

—● Tip ... To get crystal-clear ice, boil the water first and allow it to cool slightly before pouring it into the ice cube tray.

If I feel like eating a light breakfast, I opt for a smoothie. Smoothies are super quick to make and packed with nutrients. The Blueberry Swirl and Blackberry Crumble (see page 236) are quite filling, while the Ultimate Carrot, below, and the Mango Passion (see page 236) are refreshing and nourishing. Don't be wary of the red beets—when blended with berries, they taste incredible.

THE ULTIMATE CARROT SMOOTHIE

Serves 2

Ingredients

carrot juice
1 large carrot,
    peeled and chopped
1 large orange, peeled, chopped,
    and with pith removed
½ cup (125ml) coconut water
1 tbsp lemon juice

green juice
½ avocado, peeled and pitted
½ ripe banana, peeled and frozen
    a small handful of spinach
¼ cup (60ml) unsweetened
    almond milk

carrot tops, for serving

1. Combine all the carrot juice ingredients in a blender and fill 2 glasses until they are three-quarters full. Leave to one side for a couple of minutes for the pulp to naturally rise to the top. This will make it easier for the green juice to form a separate top layer.

2. Rinse the blender, then blend the green juice ingredients together. It will have a thick and creamy consistency, which will help it to float to the top.

3. Top the glasses with the green juice so that it forms a separate layer. Serve with carrot tops and straws.

RED BEET BERRY SMOOTHIE

Serves 1

Ingredients

1 raw red beet, peeled
    and chopped
a handful of raspberries
a handful of strawberries,
    hulled
1 cup (250ml) unsweetened
    almond milk

1. Combine all the ingredients in a blender and serve in a glass with 3 ice cubes.

BLUEBERRY SWIRL

Serves 2

Ingredients

banana

1 ripe banana, peeled
½ cup (50g) rolled oats
2 tbsp almond butter
1 cup (250ml) unsweetened
   almond milk

blueberry

½ cup (75g) blueberries
1 tbsp chia seeds
2 Medjool dates, pitted
   and roughly chopped

1. Make the banana smoothie first.
   Combine all the ingredients in a
   blender and pour into two glasses.

2. Next, rinse the blender and blend all
   the blueberry ingredients together
   with ¼ cup (125ml) water. Carefully
   pour the blueberry mixture over the
   banana smoothie, using a spoon to
   create a swirl on the top.

MANGO PASSION

Serves 1

Ingredients

½ mango, peeled, pitted,
   and roughly chopped
juice of ½ lime
¾ cup (180ml) coconut water
1 passion fruit, seeds and pulp
   scooped out

1. Add the mango to a blender with
   the lime juice and coconut water.
   Blend until smooth and pour into
   a glass.

2. Stir in the passion fruit seeds
   and serve.

BLACKBERRY CRUMBLE

Serves 1

Ingredients

½ cup (60g) frozen blackberries
1 apple, cored and roughly chopped
2 heaping tbsp rolled oats
1 cup (250ml) unsweetened
   almond milk
1 tsp baobab powder (optional)
1 tbsp unsalted raw almonds,
   to serve

1. Combine all the ingredients, except
   the almonds, in a blender until
   smooth and pour into a glass.

2. Crush the almonds in a mortar and
   pestle and sprinkle over the smoothie.

━━● Tip ... You can buy blackberries
and lots of other berries already frozen,
which are great for smoothies.

PRE- AND POST-WORKOUT DRINKS

What I drink on workout days hugely impacts my performance and recovery. From a pre-workout drink, I need energy and hydration, while after a workout, I want protein to help repair my muscles.

PRE-WORKOUT

ANTIOXIDANT ENERGY-BOOST SMOOTHIE

Serves 1

Ingredients

1 ripe banana, peeled
1 heaping tbsp rolled oats
¼ cup (40g) blueberries
1 tbsp raw cacao powder
½ cup (125ml) unsweetened
   almond milk

1. Add all the ingredients to a blender with ½ cup (125ml) water and blend until smooth.

PEAR + CHIA ENDURANCE JUICE

Serves 1

Ingredients

2 ripe pears, cored and
   roughly chopped
a large handful of spinach
2 celery stalks
½ cup (125ml) coconut water
1 tbsp chia seeds
1 tsp spirulina powder (optional)

1. Run the pears, spinach, and celery through a juicer.

2. Once the juicer has extracted the pulp, pour in the coconut water and stir in the chia seeds and spirulina, if using.

POST-WORKOUT

PB PROTEIN SMOOTHIE

Serves 1

Ingredients

2 tbsp hemp powder
2 tbsp smooth peanut butter
½ ripe banana, peeled
1 cup (250ml) unsweetened
   almond milk
¼ x 14-oz (400-g) can chickpeas, drained
1 tbsp raw cacao powder
½ tsp ground cinnamon
1 tsp milled flaxseed (optional)

1. Combine all the ingredients together in a blender until smooth.

RECOVERY ROOTS JUICE

Serves 1

Ingredients

6 carrots, peeled and chopped
2-inch (5-cm) piece of fresh ginger, peeled
½ tsp turmeric
1 tsp maca powder (optional)

1. Run the carrots and ginger through a juicer. Once all the pulp has been extracted, and you have the juice, stir in the turmeric and maca, if using. Drink soon after juicing.

GREEN JUICES—3 WAYS

Green juices can be a little daunting if you're new to eating healthier. So I've created three different levels of green juice: sweet for beginners; intermediate with less fruit and more vegetables; and advanced, made from 100% vegetables. All include an abundance of vital vitamins and minerals.

BEGINNER (SWEET + FRUITY)

Serves 1

Ingredients

1 cup (200g) fresh pineapple chunks
5 fresh mint leaves
2 large handfuls of spinach
½ cucumber, chopped
¼ cup (125ml) coconut water

1. Run the ingredients, except the coconut water, through a juicer.

2. Once the juicer has removed all the pulp, stir in the coconut water.

INTERMEDIATE (COOL + REFRESHING)

Serves 1

Ingredients

½ cup (125ml) coconut water
juice of ½ lemon
1 green apple, cored and
    roughly chopped
½ cucumber, chopped
½ fennel bulb, trimmed and
    roughly chopped
1-inch (2.5-cm) piece of fresh ginger, peeled

1. Set the coconut water and lemon aside and run the remaining ingredients through a juicer.

2. Once the juicer has extracted the pulp, stir in the coconut water and lemon juice.

ADVANCED (100% VEG)

Serves 1

Ingredients

½ cucumber, chopped
2 celery stalks, trimmed
2 large handfuls of kale,
  stalks removed
½ large bunch of fresh parsley,
  leaves picked
1-inch (2.5-cm) piece of fresh ginger, peeled
juice of ½ lemon

1. Gradually feed all the ingredients into a juicer, except for the lemon juice.

2. Once the juicer has extracted all the pulp, stir in the lemon juice.

━● Tip ... To get the maximum amount of juice from the kale, spinach, and herbs, compress them tightly in your hands before adding them to the juicer.

MILKSHAKES—3 WAYS

Milkshakes are not something I've had to wave goodbye to, as these wonderful naturally sweet ones are, in my opinion, far tastier than any I've ever had from fast-food restaurants. I've made these for friends, who are the biggest milk and ice cream fans, and they guzzled down my dairy-free versions, licking their lips and asking for more!

CHOCOLATE

Serves 1

Ingredients

1 cup (250ml) unsweetened
    almond milk
1 frozen banana, peeled and sliced
1 Medjool date, pitted and
    roughly chopped
1 tbsp almond butter
½ tsp ground cinnamon
½ tsp vanilla powder or 1 tsp
    organic vanilla extract
2 tsp raw cacao powder
¼ cup (25g) unsalted raw walnuts
1 tbsp raw cacao nibs

1. Add all the ingredients, except the walnuts and cacoa nibs, to a blender and blend until smooth.

2. Add the walnuts and cacao nibs and blend just until they are broken down into small chunks, but not totally smooth—we want to keep it chunky but drinkable! Pour the shake into a glass and finish with your choice of toppings.

🍇 Topping ideas ...
A teaspoon of goji berries
A teaspoon of raw cacao nibs

VANILLA

Serves 1

Ingredients

1 cup (250ml) unsweetened
    almond milk
½ tsp vanilla powder or
    1 tsp organic vanilla extract
1 parsnip, peeled and chopped
1 tsp barley malt extract
1 tbsp almond butter
1 tsp maple syrup
1 tbsp baobab powder

1. Place all the ingredients into a blender, add 2 ice cubes, and blend until smooth.

🥄 Tip ... For a smoother consistency, strain the milkshake before serving or, if you have a juicer, feed the parsnip through a juicer to get the parsnip juice beforehand.

STRAWBERRY

Serves 1

Ingredients

6 large strawberries (about 4 oz/100g),
   hulled, frozen
1 Medjool date, pitted and
   roughly chopped
½ tsp vanilla powder or 1 tsp
   organic vanilla extract
1 cup (250ml) unsweetened
   almond milk

1. Add all the ingredients to a
   blender and blend until smooth.

Tip ... Feel free to add more
strawberries for a stronger flavor.

What to
eat in a day

What I eat depends on what I'm doing. I'm usually running between meetings, filming and editing videos during the day, and then going to events in the evenings. What I eat also hugely reflects whether or not I'm doing something active—if I'm going for a run, I tend to stick to carb-heavy meals and snacks throughout the day to keep my energy levels high, whereas if I'm strength training, I focus on taking in more protein. When I'm not exercising at all, I don't need the extra energy that carbs provide and my body doesn't crave these kinds of foods.

On top of the juices and smoothies that I have listed below, I also drink about 8 cups (2 liters) of water throughout the day, every day. It's important to constantly sip slowly, rather than drink a whole glass in a couple of minutes! This way you keep your body efficiently hydrated.

WEEKEND Workout Day		
9:30am	DRINK/	**Morning Detox Drink**
10:00am	BREAKFAST/	**Coconut Pancakes with Mango Sauce**
11:30am		**Run**
1:00pm	AFTERNOON JUICE/	**Advanced Green Juice**
2:00pm	LUNCH/	**Roasted Fennel, Lentil + Fig Salad**
4:00pm	AFTERNOON SNACK/	**Root Chips + Classic Hummus**
8:30pm	DINNER/	**Italian Stuffed Peppers**
9:00pm	DESSERT/	**Black Bean Banana Brownies**

WEEKEND Chill Day		
10:30am	DRINK/	**Maple Matcha Latte**
12:00pm	BRUNCH/	**Full English Breakfast**
4:00pm	AFTERNOON SNACK/	**Oat Cakes with Strawberry Chia Jam**
8:30pm	DINNER/	**Squashetti + "Meatballs"**
9:00pm	DESSERT/	**Orange Spiced Cookies**

7:00am	BREAKFAST/ Maple Matcha Latte	WEEKDAY
	+ Banana Bread Oatmeal	Cardio Workout
8:00am	Run	
10:00am	POST-WORKOUT SMOOTHIE/ PB Protein Smoothie	
1:30pm	LUNCH/ Massaged Kale Caesar Salad	
4:00pm	AFTERNOON SNACK/ Rosemary Crackers	
	with Guacamole	
7:30pm	DINNER/ Indian Dal	
8:30pm	DESSERT/ Blueberry Burst Dates	

7:30am	BREAKFAST/ Mixed Fruit + Nut Granola with	WEEKDAY
	unsweetened almond milk + berries	Non-Workout
11:00am	LATE-MORNING SNACK/ Vanilla Milkshake	
1:00pm	LUNCH/ Raw Pea + Zucchini Soup	
3:30pm	AFTERNOON SNACK/ Sun-dried Tomato + Cashew	
	Dip with raw carrot sticks and celery stalks	
7:30pm	DINNER/ Vegetable Laksa	

7:00am	BREAKFAST/ Antioxidant Energy-Boost Smoothie	WEEKDAY
8:00am	1-hour gym strength workout	Strength
9:30am	POST-WORKOUT SNACK/ Raw Fig + Baobab Bar	Workout
11:30am	MID-MORNING SNACK/ Homemade Oat Cakes	
	with almond butter	
1:30pm	LUNCH/ Avocado + Turmeric Salad with Quinoa	
4:00pm	AFTERNOON SNACK/ Supergreen Energy Ball	
7:00pm	DINNER/ Red Beet Burgers with	
	Spiced Wedges and Summer Salsa	

Index

Page numbers in **bold** denote an illustration

ACKNOWLEDGMENTS

There are many people in my life who have made this book possible—some who have been there my whole life and some who have only been around a short while, but have nonetheless made a huge impact.

I'll start with Gleam, the team that manages me, but has become like family over the years. Dom, thank you for having faith in me from the beginning and for seeing through my crazy vision to one day have my very own cookbook, and for helping to turn that into a reality. You've always made me feel like anything is possible. Amy, I really don't know where I'd be without you! Thank you for being there and guiding me through all the incredible projects and opportunities that have emerged over our time working together, and for also being a friend.

Bronagh, thank you for always having a smile on your face and for somehow always being happy! You really do brighten even the most stressful situations. Also thank you to Abigail for being my holy grail on anything book related ... You are the coolest bookworm I know and I appreciate your invaluable knowledge!

Thank you to my wonderful publisher, HarperCollins. Grace, from the day we had our initial meeting I knew you could see my vision of *Eat Smart*. Thank you for listening and for helping me bring it to life. A huge thank you to Isabel, Lucy, Heike, and Orlando for all being absolute pleasures to work with.

Thank you to Tabbi and Alex for spending hours and hours in my kitchen,

helping me make these recipes, and for washing up the mountains of dishes that accumulated in a matter of seconds—you were an absolute godsend and you have no idea how much easier you have made the whole process. Thank you for getting me through it.

My family have always been incredibly supportive of me; whether it's a minor project I'm working on, or major life decisions, they're always there. Thank you, Mum, Paul, Grandma, Ian, and the rest of my wonderful family. And a special appreciation to my mum for always being at the other end of the phone to give me advice whenever I need her. I love you all so much!

I must also mention Marcus, who has been in my life since we were 11. From your passion for health and fitness to your entrepreneurial focus, you never fail to inspire me. I owe so much of who I am today to you, so thank you.

Thank you to all of the wonderful brands that have supplied the clothes worn throughout the book—Ralph Lauren, ASOS, Sweaty Betty, Marks & Spencer, Dune, Topshop, & Other Stories, Tommy Hilfiger, maje, Keds, and Nike.

And finally, thank you to my audience. Frankly, without you this book wouldn't be in your hands—it's all because you subscribe to me, follow me on social media, and watch my videos.

My thank you, to you, is this book, full of recipes that I have put my heart and soul into. I really hope you can tell from making my food how much love has gone into it.

STERLING EPICURE

New York

An Imprint of Sterling Publishing Co., Inc.
1166 Avenue of the Americas
New York, NY 10036

This Sterling Epicure edition published in 2017
by Sterling Publishing Co., Inc.
First published in Great Britain in 2016 by
HarperCollins*Publishers*

ISBN 978-1-4549-2686-3

Distributed in Canada by Sterling Publishing
Co., Inc.
c/o Canadian Manda Group, 664 Annette Street
Toronto, Ontario, Canada M6S 2C8

For information about custom
editions, special sales, and premium
and corporate purchases, please contact
Sterling Special Sales at 800-805-5489
or specialsales@sterlingpublishing.com.

Manufactured in China

2 4 6 8 10 9 7 5 3 1

www.sterlingpublishing.com

MIX
Paper from
responsible sources
FSC® C007454

FSC™ is a non-profit international organisation established to promote the
responsible management of the world's forests. Products carrying the FSC
label are independently certified to assure consumers that they come from
forests that are managed to meet the social, economic and ecological needs
of present and future generations, and other controlled sources.

Find out more about HarperCollins and the environment at
www.harpercollins.co.uk/green